Heroes and Villains

OSAMA BIN LADEN

Other books in the Heroes and Villains series include:

Heroes and Villains

OSAMA BIN LADEN

Bill Loehfelm

LUCENT
BOOKS®

THOMSON
━━━━✶━━━━ ™
GALE

San Diego • Detroit • New York • San Francisco • Cleveland • New Haven, Conn. • Waterville, Maine • London • Munich

LIBRARY OF CONGRESS CATALOGING-IN-PUBLICATION DATA

Loehfelm, Bill.
    Osama bin Laden / by Bill Loehfelm.
    v. cm. — (Heroes and villains)
    Includes bibliographical references and index.
    Summary: Profiles Osama bin Laden, his family background and education, his
    commitment to Islam, his mentors, the beginnings of his interest in violent and
    radical ideas, and his actions as leader of the al-Qaeda terrorist group. Includes
    discussions of war and unrest in the Middle East, including the region's growing
    resentment toward the United States.
    Contents: Shrouded in mystery—Beginnings: "like any other awkward teen-
    ager"—University: history's lessons—Afghanistan: joining the jihad—Saudi Arabia:
    "let there be no two religions in Arabia"—Sudan: one man's army—Back to
    Afghanistan: dangerous signs—Attack on America: "they will be targeted."
        ISBN 1-59018-294-4 (lib. : alk. paper)
        1. Bin Laden, Osama, 1957– 2. Terrorists—Saudia Arabia—Biography. 3.
    Violence—Religious aspects—Islam. [1. Bin Laden, Osama, 1957– 2. Terrorists.]
    I. Title. II. Heroes and villains series.
        HV6430.B55 L64 2003
        958.104'6'092—dc21   2002013066

Printed in the United States of America

Contents

Foreword

Good and evil are an ever-present feature of human history. Their presence is reflected through the ages in tales of great heroism and extraordinary villainy. Such tales provide insight into human nature, whether they involve two people or two thousand, for the essence of heroism and villainy is found in deeds rather than in numbers. It is the deeds that pique our interest and lead us to wonder what prompts a man or woman to perform such acts.

Samuel Johnson, the eminent eighteenth-century English writer, once wrote, "The two great movers of the human mind are the desire for good, and fear of evil." The pairing of desire and fear, possibly two of the strongest human emotions, helps explain the intense fascination people have with all things good and evil—and by extension, heroic and villainous.

People are attracted to the person who reaches into a raging river to pull a child from what could have been a watery grave for both, and to the person who risks his or her own life to shepherd hundreds of desperate black slaves to safety on the Underground Railroad. We wonder what qualities these heroes possess that enable them to act against self-interest, and even their own survival. We also wonder if,

under similar circumstances, we would behave as they do.

Evil, on the other hand, horrifies as well as intrigues us. Few people can look upon the drifter who mutilates and kills a neighbor or the dictator who presides over the torture and murder of thousands of his own citizens without feeling a sense of revulsion. And yet, as Joseph Conrad writes, we experience "the fascination of the abomination." How else to explain the overwhelming success of a book such as Truman Capote's *In Cold Blood*, which examines in horrifying detail a vicious and senseless murder that took place in the American heartland in the 1960s? The popularity of murder mysteries and Court TV are also evidence of the human fascination with villainy.

Most people recoil in the face of such evil. Yet most feel a deep-seated curiosity about the kind of person who could commit a terrible act. It is perhaps a reflection of our innermost fears that we wonder whether we could resist or stand up to such behavior in our presence or even if we ourselves possess the capacity to commit such terrible crimes.

The Lucent Books Heroes and Villains series capitalizes on our fascination with the perpetrators of both good and evil by introducing readers to some of history's most revered heroes and hated villains. These include heroes such as Frederick Douglass, who knew firsthand the humiliation of slavery and, at great risk to himself, publicly fought to abolish the institution of slavery in America. It also includes villains such as Adolf Hitler, who is remembered both for the devastation of Europe and for the murder of 6 million Jews and thousands of Gypsies, Slavs, and others whom Hitler deemed unworthy of life.

Each book in the Heroes and Villains series examines the life story of a hero or villain from history. Generous use of primary and secondary source quotations gives readers eyewitness views of the life and times of each individual as well as enlivens the narrative. Notes and annotated bibliographies provide stepping-stones to further research.

SHROUDED IN MYSTERY

As the United States began the long task of recovering from the devastation of September 11, the name of one man was on everyone's lips: Osama bin Laden, the most feared and reviled terrorist on the planet. The forty-four-year-old Saudi exile caught the world's attention in the most horrific manner possible, by orchestrating the September 11, 2001, attacks.

Osama bin Laden was not always the man he is now. He began his life with much good fortune. He was born into a wealthy family, with every comfort and convenience available. A future of high education, international business concerns, and continued wealth and comfort awaited him. What drove him to undertake a mission directing bombings and hijackings from a mountain cave is still elusive. What is more

Osama bin Laden masterminded the devastating terrorist attacks in the United States on September 11, 2001.

clear is that bin Laden has demonstrated, since long before the September 11 attacks, a fearsome commitment to striking at the "infidels" he feels plague his part of the world. In fulfilling this commitment, he has shown a reach that extends far beyond the Middle East.

What made Osama bin Laden the man he is may never be fully known. Nevertheless, there are events in his life that undoubtedly influenced him. His mother, who was not a devout Muslim, was scorned by his family. His father died when bin Laden was eleven. His oldest brother was killed in a plane crash. During his late teens and early twenties, bin Laden's Arab homeland experienced great turmoil.

Since the deaths of his father and brother, bin Laden has been influenced by older, more experienced men: Abdullah Azzam in college and Afghanistan; radical clerics in Saudi Arabia; Ayman al-Zawahiri, an Egyptian physician and terrorist; the leaders of Hamas and Hezbollah in Sudan; al-Qaeda's military leader, Mohammed Atef; and Mullah Omar, the leader of the Taliban. Bin Laden has always known how to use both his religion and his money to win loyalty from others: the Afghan mujahideen, the government of Sudan, the Taliban, leaders of the world's terrorist groups, and his thousands of recruits, followers, and supporters. Throughout his development as a terrorist, he has used the business and financial skills he learned from his family.

Al-Qaeda

What some feel is bin Laden's crowning accomplishment was his ability to turn al-Qaeda into the massive yet elusive terrorist force that it is. He did so relatively unchecked by those he had publicly sworn to attack. Al-Qaeda was active in the United States for ten years before September 11. It has had active operatives throughout Europe, Africa, and Asia for many years. It is only in the last year that the public has become aware of the true reach of al-Qaeda. How much farther that reach extends and what else al-Qaeda may reach out to strike is still being determined and remains largely unknown.

The hallmark of al-Qaeda, however, is neither its reach nor its destructiveness; rather, it is the sheer number of men from whom bin Laden has been able to gain utter loyalty. Al-Qaeda members, of which there are thousands, will readily and enthusiastically lay down their lives for him. Nineteen men willingly died on September 11 in the service of bin Laden's cause. There were others before the 9/11 hijackers and there have been many since. Though bin Laden has maintained his commitment to his cause, his organization has been so effective because of its members' loyalty to him.

A New Enemy

Bin Laden holds a unique place in the list of America's enemies, both past and present. Never before has the United

States, now the world's superior military force, put its considerable might behind the defeat of a single man. Osama bin Laden is not a king or an emperor, nor does he lead a country. In the past, America has always waged its wars against other nations. Never before has it waged war against an organization and its leader. This fact considerably complicates the search for bin Laden, who has been in hiding since October 2001. Since he is not part of the formal structure of a particular nation, there is no capital to corner him in, no ports to

Muslims in a mass rally in Kashmir, Pakistan, show their loyalty to Osama bin Laden, the leader of al-Qaeda.

blockade, no borders across which to mount an invasion. Bin Laden is a man with hidden allies and secret hiding places in several different countries.

However, bin Laden faces several disadvantages because of his isolation. He has no national economy to bankroll his war. He cannot build his own weapons. He has no real scientific or technological systems through which to advance and improve his capabilities. He has no formal military to defend him. More than ever, he has to scrounge for the basic necessities such as food, water, and shelter. Unlike with any villain in history, no nation is his ally. In fact, most of the world has joined in the U.S. pursuit of him. Therefore, just as there are great challenges in bringing bin Laden to justice, bin Laden himself faces great challenges in his attempts to remain free.

Uncertain Future

Whatever becomes of him, Osama bin Laden has reminded the world of painful facts. There are people who still believe that violence and hatred are acceptable, admirable, and effective ways to achieve goals. He has reminded the world that there are also people willing to follow a violent and vengeful leader, people who are willing to commit murder but do not fear their own death. Bin Laden has proved to the world that it no longer takes a nation to start a war.

What effect the capture or death of Osama bin Laden will have on global terrorism can only be speculated. Some believe that, because of his superiority as a leader, no one can replace him and al-Qaeda would disintegrate without him. No one knows for sure whether bin Laden will ever be heard from again, or if he is, how he will deliver that message. Perhaps only bin Laden himself, if he is indeed still alive, knows what his future holds. All that is certain is that Osama bin Laden has left his black mark on history, and while he will be remembered as a hero by some, he will be remembered as a villain by most.

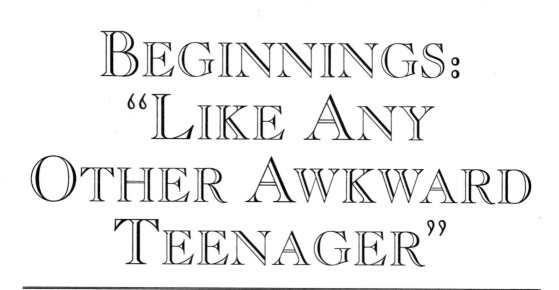

BEGINNINGS: "LIKE ANY OTHER AWKWARD TEENAGER"

Osama bin Mohammed bin Laden was born on July 30, 1957, in Riyadh, Saudi Arabia, to Mohammed bin Laden and his wife Hamida. He was the seventeenth son born to Mohammed and one of his many wives. In 1964, the bin Laden family moved from Riyadh to Medina and later to the city of Jeddah. Although the family remained in Jeddah for the rest of Osama's childhood, they also spent significant amounts of time in the Muslim holy cities of Mecca and Medina.

Osama, whose first name means "young lion," is one of fifty children, and his family is one of the richest in Saudi Arabia. Mohammed bin Laden's construction and engineering company,

the Bin Laden Group, was worth over $1 billion by the time Osama was born. As he grew up, Osama's early experiences with his family, his religion, and the Arab world caused conflicting feelings within him.

Humble Beginnings

Osama bin Laden's father, Mohammed, came from very humble beginnings. He grew up in the impoverished Hadramaut province of Yemen, a small Middle Eastern nation south of Saudi Arabia. He was born in a tiny village named al-Rubat, seated in the valley of Wadi Doan. It was an area very isolated from the outside world and was considered primitive. Mohammed received no education beyond lessons in Islam and never learned to read or write. He never even learned to sign his name.

As a young man with no school to attend, Mohammed sought work. His first job was in construction, working as a bricklayer for an Arab-American oil company. He made the equivalent of fifteen cents a day. Even though he was uneducated, Mohammed was intelligent and industrious. He labored long hours and saved his money. Because al-Rubat was so poor, many of its young men left the valley and even left Yemen to go find work. Mohammed followed the same path.

Eventually, he and his brother immigrated to Jeddah, Saudi Arabia, an arduous trip of over a hundred miles.

Mohammed planned to start his own construction company in Saudi Arabia. But he needed money to get the company started, so Mohammed first found work as a porter in a busy Jeddah hotel. Jeddah, located near the holy city of Mecca, was a popular stop for the millions of Islamic pilgrims visiting Mecca every year. While working at the hotel, Mohammed became friends with members of the al-Saud family, who also made their living entertaining visitors to Jeddah. Only two years later, the al-Sauds

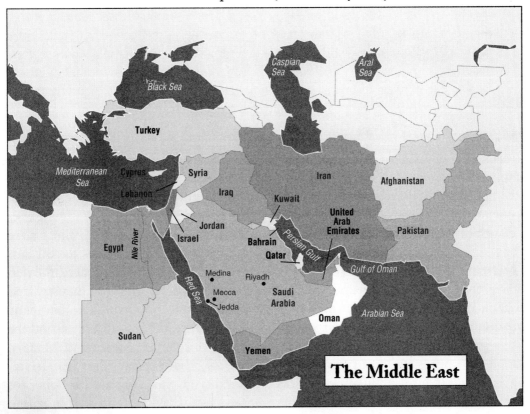

The Middle East

Saudi Arabia: Origins of a Modern Kingdom

The modern nation of Saudi Arabia, as it is seen and heard about in the news today, was created not long ago. The Kingdom of Saudi Arabia, with its current borders and government, was formed in 1932. The government is a monarchy: A king rules and is advised by an appointed parliament. When a king dies, his successor is selected from the royal family. The laws of Islam are declared to be the official laws of the kingdom. Since the country's creation, it has been ruled by the al-Saud family. Abd al-Aziz ibn al-Saud, also called Ibn Saud, was Saudi Arabia's first king.

Attempts to unify the Arabian Peninsula, the landmass that makes up Saudi Arabia, began in the eighteenth century. The Wahhabi, a group of strict Muslims seeking to unify Arabia, formed an alliance with the powerful al-Saud family. This alliance was supported by the peninsula's large Bedouin population, a tribe of desert nomads. These three groups were able to unite Arabia under Islamic rule from 1811 to 1818.

In 1818, Arabia was conquered by Egypt. The Wahhabis rose again in the mid–nineteenth century, only to again be conquered—this time by the Rashid dynasty. The Wahhabis survived, however, and returned to power in Arabia in the early twentieth century. They were led this time by Ibn Saud, who was descended from the original Wahhabi rulers of Arabia. Saud conquered all of Arabia by 1925, and by 1932 he had formed the kingdom his family still rules today.

became Saudi Arabia's royal and ruling family. Mohammed's friendships with the family would prove beneficial to his construction company, which he founded with his brother in 1931.

Turning Bricks into Gold

Over the next twenty years, the Bin Laden Group, Mohammed's construction company, grew into a large and successful business. Mohammed developed an impressive reputation as an efficient and honest businessman as well as a devout Muslim. He could fin-

ish projects faster than other contractors, do better quality work, and account for every "riyal," the smallest unit of Saudi currency.

By the early 1950s, the Bin Laden Group was building palaces for the ruling al-Sauds, who had accumulated enormous wealth in the oil industry, and became quite powerful. The company won a contract to restore and expand the Great Mosques in Mecca and Medina, two of the holiest sites in Islam. Working on them was a great honor for the devout Mohammed. He often prayed at the mosques he helped rebuild.

Rebuilding the mosques brought Mohammed and his company increased respect from the al-Sauds. The Bin Laden Group became the exclusive contractor of the royal family. More contracts and more money flooded in to the bin Laden business, thus increasing the bin Laden family's own wealth. Through their many business dealings, the al-Saud and bin Laden families maintained close personal ties.

In the early 1960s, Mohammed won a bid to build a massive highway linking the cities of Jeddah and Medina. When completed, the highway stretched all the way across the country. It was a massive and symbolic achievement for the man who had arrived in Jeddah thirty-five years earlier as a poor and humble laborer.

A Stern Father

Mohammed bin Laden was raised in al-Rubat under a strict and conservative form of Islam called Sunni. Daily prayers were very important, and shops closed at prayer time. Sunni has strict rules governing contact between men and women. Mohammed grew up in a community where women were not allowed to work or even drive. Because

Muslims kneel in prayer. As a devout Muslim, Mohammed bin Laden felt honored that his construction company restored the Great Mosques in Mecca and Medina.

complete honesty was so important to Sunni Muslims, Mohammed's religious beliefs greatly benefited his business. He maintained his strong faith his entire life. When he became a husband and father, he insisted that all of his many children be raised Sunni. Mohammed was the first religious influence on young Osama.

Though often away at work and rarely with his family, Mohammed had a powerful influence on his household. All his children lived under one roof until they were adults. Mohammed demanded of them the same devotion to Islam he had learned as a child and continued as an adult. They were all raised in the Sunni tradition. All the children would pray and read the Koran, the Muslim holy book, before going to school. Because of the Sunni rules governing contact between men and women, the sons could not show their faces to the female maids. Mohammed insisted his children show discipline and confidence, and all of his sons were brought up to eventually be part of the family business.

When Mohammed bin Laden was killed in a 1968 helicopter crash, the year Osama turned eleven, he left to his family a business empire that was world-renowned and worth billions of dollars. Osama's oldest brother, Salem, took over the business and carried on his father's wishes that all the bin Laden sons have a place in the Bin Laden Group. To this day, the bin

Laden family's corporation, which has since expanded to include a range of companies beyond construction, remains one of the most successful businesses in Saudi Arabia and one of the biggest and most influential in the Arab world.

Woman of Another World

Osama's mother, Hamida, came from a large, influential family of her own. However, by the time Hamida, at age twenty-two, married Mohammed bin Laden, she had already lived a very different life than her husband. The beautiful daughter of a Syrian trader, Hamida grew up in a wealthy family and was well educated. Though she was a Muslim, she shunned many of the Muslim social traditions concerning how women should live. Instead of wearing the traditional attire consisting of robes and veils, Hamida favored expensive pantsuits and makeup. She had traveled outside the Middle East and was considerably more modern and worldly than her husband.

Hamida had little status in the bin Laden family. As is the Muslim tradition, Hamida was one of several wives taken by Mohammed. Because of her nontraditional ways, and because she was Syrian and not Saudi, Hamida was regarded as little more than a temporary servant by Mohammed's three permanent Saudi wives. Though Osama and the other children lived at the main bin Laden residence, Hamida was not permitted to live there. At any

Muslim women in traditional garb. Osama bin Laden's mother Hamida preferred to wear contemporary dress.

time, Mohammed could dissolve the marriage, leave Hamida with nothing if he wanted, and replace her with a new wife. By contrast, she had little say even in the upbringing of her own children. It was Mohammed who made the rules and the permanent wives who taught them to the children.

The marriage did not last long. Mohammed divorced Hamida a few years before his death. Though they had Osama and several daughters together, Hamida never bore Mohammed another son. This is thought to be the main reason for the divorce, since sons were viewed as much more important than daughters in the bin Laden family. As soon as they were divorced, Hamida was no longer considered part of the

bin Laden family. She did, however, remain in close contact with Osama as he was growing up and into his adult life.

Beginnings of Devotion

Osama was greatly affected by his mother's low place in the family. He was aware of the fact that, unlike his father's other wives, Hamida had only been "allowed" to conceive a single son. He was ashamed that his mother had been effectively kicked out of the family for failing in her duties as a Muslim woman. Osama saw his mother as being punished for her Western ways, for not being devout enough in her faith. Even though he remained close to Hamida, the lack of respect shown to his mother by the rest of the family strengthened

Osama's commitment to Islamic tradition. He began questioning the West's influence on Islamic culture, believing it had damaged his family.

In addition to his father's devotion and his mother's shame, there were other influences on young Osama's religious development. The bin Laden family's close ties with the royal family put them in regular contact with Saudi Arabia's religious elite. Muslims from around the world stayed at the bin Laden house during their hajj, the pilgrimage to Mecca required by Islam of its followers. Young Osama had plenty

Muslim pilgrims throng the Great Mosque at Mecca.

of opportunities to talk with many Muslim clerics, scholars, and teachers. To him, devotion to Islam produced wise and powerful men.

Of all the bin Laden children, Osama stood out as particularly devoted to Islam and his father's teachings, even at an early age. It was not unusual for a preteen Osama to spend extra time in prayer. He devoted many hours to reading and learning the words of the Koran. He asked many questions of his siblings and the household visitors concerning the teachings of the holy book. While his other siblings played, and while his brothers began learning the family business, young Osama continued to focus his attention on Islam. In a 2002 interview with CNN, Osama's brother Sheik Ahmed spoke of Osama's devotion to his religion:

> When we were very young, he would wake up me and my sister. We were lazy, we were young, but we had to get up; he was our older brother. He would say "Ahmed, get up, get up," and we would. We would pray with him and then just go to school, without going back to sleep.[1]

A Courteous and Confident Youth

Osama also stood out from other young people at school. As an early teen, Osama was an excellent student.

He studied at the prestigious al-Thagh school in Jeddah, a small, Western-style school where his classmates were other privileged and intelligent Saudi boys. Osama impressed his teachers as a humble and conscientious student, handing in work that was neat and precise. According to Brian Fyfield-Shayler, Osama's English teacher when he was thirteen, the young man also stood out for other reasons:

> He was very courteous—more so than any of the other boys in his class. Physically, he was outstanding because he was taller, more hand-some and fairer than most of the other boys. He also stood out as he was singularly gracious and polite, and had a great deal of inner confidence.[2]

As a teenager in the late 1960s and early 1970s, Osama lived a life typical of his family and his age. He went to the movies with his brothers; westerns and karate movies were his favorites. He also appeared comfortable with his family's wealth and joined them on vacations to Sweden and England, where he and his brothers showed off their expensive clothes, cars, and jewelry. There are pho-tos of Osama in the fashionable clothes of the time. One summer, the family flew a Rolls-Royce from Saudi Arabia to Denmark to use during a vacation.

Christina Akerblad owned the Astoria Hotel, where the bin Laden family stayed while in Sweden. She remem-bers the bin Laden sons well: "They had lots of white silk shirts packaged in cellophane. I think they had a new one for every day—I never saw the dirty ones. They also had a big bag for their jewelry. They had emeralds and rubies and diamond rings and tie pins."[3]

In 1971, following the family tradi-tion, Osama went to an exclusive lan-guage school in Oxford, England. Osama learned numerous languages at the school and become acclimated to living in an international community. According to *Salon* magazine's Jason Burke, there is a photo of bin Laden from the summer of 1971 that shows him "wearing flares, a short-sleeved shirt and a bracelet, looking like any other awkward teenager." While in school, he played sports, flirted with girls, and made many friends. "In bin Laden's early teens, there was little sign of the fanatic he was to become."[4]

Oil Fields and Battlefields

While Osama was living the normal life of a wealthy teen, much of his native Arab world was changing. By the late 1960s, many Muslims felt that the United States, for decades a major industrial presence in the Middle East because of oil, had too much political, economic, and cultural influence. Many Muslims began calling for increased Arab political and economic indepen-dence. Western culture, viewed as immoral, money-hungry, and corrupt,

Islam

Islam is the youngest of the world's three dominant religions that center on a belief in a single supreme god. (The other two religions are Judaism and Christianity.) In Islam, the supreme god's name is Allah. Followers of Islam are called Muslims. *Muslim* is an Arabic word that means "one who submits." Followers of Islam are expected to submit to the will and teachings of Allah in all things. Belief in Allah and submission to his teachings is the primary rule of Islam. The other main rules (or pillars) of Islam are *salah*, the five daily prayers; *zakat*, giving alms to the poor; *hajj*, a pilgrimage to the holy city of Mecca; and *sawm*, the sunrise-to-sunset fast during the Muslim holy month of Ramadan.

Islam was started in the seventh century A.D. by a forty-year-old Arabian business-man named Muhammad. Muhammad believed he was called by Allah to write down Allah's wishes, wisdom, and commands for the human race to follow. Muhammad made these writings into a holy book called the Koran. Muhammad, sometimes referred to as the Prophet, set about teaching the ways of Islam to others. His teachings were rejected by many, sometimes violently. There are many tales of Muhammad fighting back against unbelievers, so he is regarded as a warrior as well as a prophet and a teacher. In the century after Muhammad's death, Islam spread across Arabia, Africa, and Asia and into Europe. Millions of people converted to Islam.

The Koran is the central text of Islam. It contains the revelations granted to Muhammad by Allah. In addition to the Koran, there are many holy writings about the words and deeds of Muhammad, called the hadith. The Koran, the hadith, and writings that interpret and explain the hadith form the holy texts of Islam.

An Afghan boy studies the Koran.

was seen by many Arabs as overpowering and destroying traditional Islamic culture. As a result, pro-Islam political and religious movements soon emerged in Arab nations such as Egypt, Jordan, Syria, Lebanon, and Saudi Arabia.

The Arab-Israeli wars of 1967 and 1973 helped increase mistrust and anger toward the United States. In the Six-Day War of 1967, Egypt, Jordan, and Syria tried to invade the Jewish nation of Israel. The Arab forces were not only quickly defeated but each nation lost territory to Israel. The United States supported Israel during this war, angering many Muslims. In 1970, five Arab nations met in Cairo, Egypt, and agreed to continue fighting for Israeli-occupied lands. This agreement led to the second Arab-Israeli war, the Yom Kippur War, which began in 1973. The forces of Egypt, Syria, and Iraq were defeated by the Israelis in 1974, and more Arab lands were annexed by Israel. Again, the United States supported Israel in this war and Arab resentment of the United States increased.

Leadership changes in the Arab world also led to resentment toward the United States. In 1970, Colonel Muammar Qaddafi assumed control of the Arab nation of Libya and formed a strict Islamic dictatorship that espoused anti-Western beliefs. He expelled from Libya oil companies and government representatives from the United States, calling for Arab nations to resist U.S. influence. In 1972, Iran's shah, backed

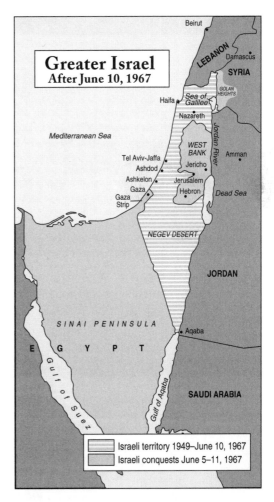

Greater Israel
After June 10, 1967

Israeli territory 1949–June 10, 1967
Israeli conquests June 5–11, 1967

by the United States, established a dictatorship in Iran that many felt was too friendly with the West. Many Muslims believed that the United States was trying to rule an Arab nation by aiding a dictatorship. U.S. support of the shah turned more Muslims against the United States.

The growing anti-American sentiment in the Middle East placed Saudi Arabia in a difficult position. As a major oil-producing nation, Saudi Arabia had

The Arab-Israeli Conflicts

The conflict between Israelites and Arabs goes back to ancient times. Though the conflict is often viewed as a religious battle between Jews and Muslims, it started as a fight for the land between the Mediterranean's eastern shores and the Jordan River. The conflict began before Islam ever existed. Both sides claim to be the land's original settlers and claim that it is their ancestral home. The Arabs, most of whom are now Muslim, came to dominate the Middle East, and the Israelites, the original Jewish people, were dispersed across Europe. The long-contested area became known as Palestine.

At the very end of the nineteenth century, talk began in Switzerland of creating a Jewish homeland in Palestine. After World War I, when sections of Palestine were under British control, European Jews were invited to settle there. In the 1920s and 1930s, hundreds of thousands of Jews moved to Palestine. The Palestinians felt that their land was being invaded by an ancient enemy, and violent clashes began immediately. In 1947, Britain surrendered the still violent area to the United Nations. In 1948, the Jewish state of Israel was created within borders established by the UN. The UN created no new state for the Palestinians. The Palestinians resented this and immediately sought to destroy the new state. To them, the bullies of the West had handed over Palestinian land to their enemy.

Arab nations such as Egypt and Syria took up the cause of the Palestinians in the 1960s, leading to the Arab-Israeli wars, wars that ultimately ended up increasing the size of Israel. The Palestinians remained without a government or a nation. In the 1970s, Yasser Arafat created the Palestinian Liberation Organization (PLO), which was supposed to lead the way in the creation of a Palestinian state. Arafat sought to regain lost land and used terrorism against Israel in the hopes that the nation would surrender land for the planned Palestinian state. The turn to terrorism gave the ancient conflict the face it wears today.

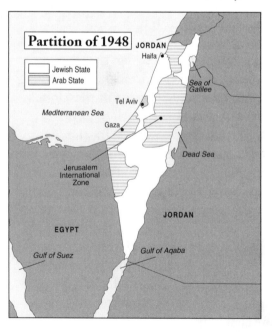

strong ties with the United States that it wanted to maintain. The United States bought most of Saudi Arabia's oil. However, Saudi Arabia also wanted to remain friendly with its increasingly anti-U.S. neighbors such as Iraq, Syria, and Egypt. The citizens of Saudi Arabia began to pressure the ruling family to choose sides. Wealthy businesspeople wanted to maintain the country's profitable relationship with the United States. Meanwhile, many cultural and religious leaders wanted Saudi Arabia to return to a society dominated by the laws and traditions of Islam.

Conflicting Loyalties

Now in his midteens, Osama bin Laden was greatly affected by the growing conflicts in his country and the surrounding regions. He felt that Arabs were being exploited for labor and oil and that the West corrupted Islam with casual morals and money. According to Burke, "the very things that had made the father huge riches began to trouble the son."[5]

Bin Laden began to turn against the Western culture he embraced as a younger boy, no longer going to movies or listening to music with his brothers. He began growing a beard and abandoned European fashions for more traditional Saudi dress such as robes and

turbans. Even more of his time was spent studying and discussing Islam. Among friends and family, bin Laden voiced his suspicions of the West and his fears concerning the future of Islam in Saudi Arabia and across the Middle East.

Bin Laden's increasingly hostile attitude toward the West set him at odds with his family. He feared his family was being pulled away from the teachings of Islam and was concerned about their continued involvement with the West. Salem, his oldest brother, went to boarding school in England. Another brother, Yeslam, went on to study in Sweden and California. Other members of the bin Laden family settled in Miami, Florida. (Osama himself never set foot in the United States.)

In 1974, when bin Laden was seventeen, he made a major break from his family tradition in favor of Islamic tradition. However, when it was time for him to go to college, bin Laden agreed to study management and economics. He was still willing to take a place in the family business. He did, however, insist on attending a Muslim university in Saudia Arabia. His reason for this decision was clear. Bin Laden would please his family but only in a way that would allow him to further his study of and devotion to Islam.

Chapter Two

UNIVERSITY: HISTORY'S LESSONS

In 1975, Osama bin Laden began classes at King Abdul Aziz University in Jeddah, Saudi Arabia. His enrollment at the Saudi university served several purposes. The university was a place where bin Laden could study the subjects his family wanted him to learn. However, it also allowed him the opportunity to remain in a Muslim community where he could further his studies of Islam. In addition, bin Laden could remain in Saudi Arabia during what he felt was an increasingly important time in both Saudi and Arab history. At the university, bin Laden grew further away from his family as important events in the Middle East attracted him to radical people and actions.

A New Community

Attending King Abdul Aziz University had an immediate impact on bin Laden. The university was an inspiring place for a young, restless Muslim like Osama bin Laden. Bin Laden found many people there who were also unhappy about what they saw as the dwindling importance of Islam in the Middle East. Bin Laden found himself in a community that shared his interest in and devotion to a strict Islamic way of life.

Interest in fundamentalist Islam had been growing for years throughout the Middle East. Many people saw a return to fundamentalist Islam as a solution to the poverty and political corruption that had plagued many

Muslim nations for a long time. It was also seen as a way to fight the corrupting influence of the non-Muslim societies of Europe and America. As the movement spread throughout the Middle East, some people involved began to view war and violence as the best way to spread their message and to save Islam, in some cases from its own leaders.

When bin Laden arrived in Jeddah, the place where his father had begun to build his empire, it was in the midst of a genuine social movement. Teachers as well as students were getting behind the fundamentalist movement. According to Jason Burke of *Salon*,

Jedda itself—and King Abdul Aziz University—[were] a center for Islamic dissidents from all over the world.... They preached a severe message: only an absolute return to the values of conservative Islam could protect the Muslim World from the dangers and decadence of the West.[6]

Brothers at Odds

As bin Laden began college amid a radical underground, his family still had hopes that he would take an important place in the family business. During high school, bin Laden had

Many in the Middle East are studying fundamentalist Islam. Here, Afghans pore over the Koran.

The Saudi Bin Laden Group

Although Osama bin Laden turned away from the family business in order to pursue his war with the West and his dream of a Khalifate, the Saudi Bin Laden Group (SBG) continues to be run by his family. Osama's oldest brother, Salem, was killed in a 1988 plane crash over San Antonio, Texas, but his other brothers remain in all the top administrative positions of SBG. The company continues to be a formidable business concern in the Middle East and the rest of the world.

As of 1999, the main company, the SBG construction business, was worth over $5 billion and employed thirty-seven thousand people. The family has diversified the business, so it is now involved in dozens of undertakings, from manufacturing to resort management. A bin Laden company is also the Middle East distributor of Porsche and Volkswagen.vehicles. SBG has built hotels and resorts in Jordan and Syria, as well as an airport and suburban housing in Egypt. Ironically, SBG also built an American military base in Saudi Arabia.

Up until the September 11 attacks, many members of the bin Laden family lived in the United States. Though all have since returned to Europe or the Middle East, SBG remains a presence in America. The family owns property in Texas and New Jersey. There is an architecture scholarship at Harvard University that bears the family name. They have an American law firm, and they continue to do business in the Middle East with such American-based corporations as Disney, Snapple, and the Hard Rock Café.

worked for the family company, sometimes even laboring on road crews. Though he moved from the desert roadside to air-conditioned offices, he continued learning how to manage a business. Bin Laden agreed to study management and economics in addition to Arab history and Islamic studies. He worked toward a degree in public administration. His eldest brother, Salem, who had taken over the bin Laden corporation in the wake of Mohammed bin Laden's death, made sure that civil

engineering was a key component of Osama's coursework at the university.

Salem, who renamed the family company the Saudi Bin Laden Group (SBG), only further alienated Osama from the family. Osama thought his older brother was leading the family away from Islam. Salem married an English woman who was not Muslim, piloted his own fleet of private jets, and played guitar. He also became close friends with King Fahd of Saudi Arabia, just as Osama felt the Saudi government was becoming dangerously Westernized.

While Osama studied at the university, Salem increased the bin Laden family's associations with the United States, a nation Osama continued to view with growing mistrust and suspicion. SBG did business in Houston, Texas, where they purchased an airport. Salem bought a vacation home in Orlando, Florida. Such moves helped increase the profits and international prestige of SBG, but the more intimate his family became with the United States, the less Osama wanted to be a part of SBG. CNN correspondent Peter Bergen, author of *Holy War, Inc.*, writes, "While Salem was taking over the family business, Osama was showing increasing signs of the religiosity that has marked his life."[7]

As his college years went on, the study of Islam became even more important to Osama bin Laden. He became deeply involved in campus religious activities. He attended prayer groups and religious debates and studied the Koran with friends. He also joined a group called the Muslim Brotherhood, a radical group that shared bin Laden's desire to live in an Arab world ruled by Islamic law and free of Western corruption. The little time he spent at home was devoted to solitary prayer. According to bin Laden's brother Abdelaziz, Osama was "reading and praying all the time"[8] during his college years.

Radical Voices

While pursuing his study of Islam and furthering his dedication to the religion, bin Laden came across the teachings of two men who would have a profound influence on him. These men, Abdullah Azzam and Muhammad Qutb, were considered respected teachers of Islamic studies by some and feared as dangerous radicals by others. By the time their teachings reached Osama bin Laden, Azzam and Qutb had already attracted many young followers throughout Saudi Arabia and the rest of the Arab world.

Born in Palestine and educated in Syria, Azzam grew up a lifelong hater of Israel. He fought with the Syrian army in the Arab-Israeli war of 1967. After the war, he studied Islamic law in Egypt. For a short while he taught Islamic studies in Jordan, but he was fired for criticizing the school's administration for a lack of devotion to true Islam. After leaving Jordan, Azzam moved to Saudi Arabia to teach.

By the time of his arrival in Saudi Arabia, Azzam was already known as a revolutionary. At one time, he was a close associate of Yasser Arafat, the leader of the Palestinian Liberation Organization. This organization wanted to lead the Palestinian communities that neighbor Israel to independent statehood. It is often blamed for introducing terrorism into the Arab-Israeli conflict. In addition to this contact, Azzam was already associated with

Abdullah Azzam was once a close associate of Palestinian leader Yasser Arafat (pictured).

Islamic extremists in Egypt and had been expelled from that country. Bin Laden discovered his teachings via audiotapes given to him by friends at the university. He was excited by Azzam's claims that the Arab world could be saved by "the rifle alone: no conferences, no negotiations and no dialogues."[9] He believed there was no future for Islam without jihad, a holy war against non-Muslims. Abdullah Azzam became the most influential figure in bin Laden's life.

In the mid-1970s, Muhammad Qutb was already known and respected in the Middle East as an Islamic scholar. He was the brother of Sayyid Qutb, a famed Islamic radical and writer. Sayyid wrote *Signposts*, the most important book of the growing radical Islamic movement. Muhammad took over the teaching of his brother's writings after

Sayyid was executed by the Egyptian government in 1966.

Like Azzam, Muhammad Qutb also advocated a movement in which devout Muslims seek out and destroy what Qutb called "the enemies of Islam, whether they be non-Islamic societies or Muslim societies that are not following the precepts of the Koran."[10] Qutb believed that Muslims were in a state of ignorance, called *jahilyyah*, equal to the days before the revelations of the Koran and the start of Islam. To Qutb, jihad was the only way out of this state and the only way back to true Islam. *Signposts*, and its ideas, as interpreted by Muhammad Qutb, became almost as important to bin Laden as the Koran.

Both Azzam and Qutb preached very radical and violent views about the role of Islam and the duty of Muslims in the future of Arabia. They believed in an offensive jihad, one in which Muslims attacked their enemies first. They taught their followers, Osama bin Laden now among them, that all non-Muslims, and Muslims who were not appropriately devout, must be killed or expelled from the Arab world by violence. All Muslims, they preached, could one day be united under a single leader. This state would be called a Khalifate. It was from these men that Osama bin Laden first heard the idea

Bin Laden's Islam

As Islam has spread around the world, it has been brought into hundreds of nations and thousands of cultures. Because of this, there are now innumerable different versions, interpretations, and practices of the religion. Dozens of different varieties of Islam can exist in the same nation. Just as there are different strains of Christianity and Judaism, so are there different strains of Islam. Nearly all widely practiced versions of Islam, however, embrace the tolerance and compassion instructed in the Koran.

It has been noted by some scholars that Osama bin Laden's actions betray even the strict, fundamentalist form of Islam, Sunni, that he was raised to practice. For example, Muslim scholars have mentioned how, often, bin Laden's interpretation of the Koran, such as his definition of *jihad*, and his actions, primarily the practice of terrorism, contradict the most basic ideals of the religion he says he is trying to save. It is a widely held belief by Muslim scholars that bin Laden interprets the Koran to suit his needs, instead of shaping his life according to the teachings of the Koran. For example, while the Koran encourages spreading Islam to unbelievers, nowhere does it sanction conversion by threat, fear, or force. And while Muslims are permitted to defend themselves with force, the Koran never states that it is permissible to kill civilians.

Though bin Laden declares Jews and Christians the enemies of Islam, and has advocated and practiced their murder, "the People of the Book" are specifically cited for tolerance in the Koran. Islam accepts many of the same traditions as Judaism and Christianity and reveres important figures in those religions, such as Abraham, Moses, and Jesus, as holy men and prophets.

that jihad was the obligation of all Muslims, an idea that greatly appealed to him.

Unwelcome at Home

As bin Laden's interest in violent and radical ideas grew in the late '70s, he began to bring his ideas home. He would share his ideas about jihad and a Khalifate with his brothers. He would preach the teachings of Azzam and Qutb to friends of the family. As the bin Ladens' personal and business associations with the Saudi ruling family grew, Osama became more openly critical of both that relationship and the Saudi government.

His ideas and teachings were not welcomed by his family. His brothers urged him to give up his radical views and return to the family business. They believed that Osama was beginning a hopeless quest to create what amounted to a Muslim fairy tale. They urged him to instead concentrate on a future with SBG. Bin Laden ignored their pleas. The more his brothers pushed him to change direction, the more committed Osama became to jihad and the Khalifate. "Like tens of thousands of other young men in the region at the time," writes Jason Burke, "Osama became increasingly drawn to the cool, clear, uncluttered certainties of extremist Islamist ideology."[11]

Year of Change

In 1979, the start of a new century in the Muslim calendar, while a twenty-two-year-old Osama bin Laden was nearing the end of his formal education, the Middle East was shaken by several events of major importance. These events changed the face of the Middle East, influenced the entire world, and inspired bin Laden, along with thousands of like-minded young radicals throughout the Middle East, to put his dreams of jihad into action. "These events," writes Benjamin Orbach, "provided [bin Laden] with a purpose he had previously lacked in his life."[12]

The first event was a January political uprising led by Islamic militants in Iran. The shah of Iran was overthrown. The Ayatollah Khomeini, a hard-line

The Ayatollah Khomeini (with white beard) was instrumental in ousting the shah of Iran, a political event that influenced bin Laden's thinking.

Muslim cleric, returned to Iran's capital city of Tehran and seized power. He established a religious dictatorship and imposed strict Islamic law as the law of the land. Bin Laden and his compatriots saw this coup as a defeat of the West and were excited by the establishment of a state ruled by Islamic law. They began to believe that what had happened in Iran was possible in other countries. A change in Egypt, however, disappointed Islamic radicals around the world.

In 1979, Egypt signed a peace agreement with Israel. Egypt had long been regarded by Muslims as an Arab leader and an Arab superpower. It had led the wars against Israel in 1967 and 1973. The signing of the peace treaty angered Muslims throughout the Middle East, Osama bin Laden among them. Many Muslims still hungered for the destruction of the Jewish state, which they believed was founded on stolen Arab land. They felt betrayed by Egypt and were suspicious of the role the United States had played in reaching the peace agreement. Bin Laden believed that the West had tricked another Arab government into betraying Islam.

Trouble in Saudi Arabia

The unrest that was brewing throughout the Middle East soon came to Saudi Arabia. Although billions of dollars had poured into the country, mostly due to the oil trade with the United States, only a select few Saudis benefited from the flow of wealth. The al-Saud family benefited the most. Many people felt that the al-Sauds had neglected their duties as leaders to concentrate on the business of getting rich. As resentment grew among the general population, unemployment, illiteracy, and poverty remained high. Many Saudis still had trouble getting fresh drinking water.

Many Saudis resented and feared the royal family's close ties to the United States, which was perceived as decadent and lawless. There were fears that Islamic law, the law on which the nation was founded, was being undermined by the corrupting influence of the Americans. The perception that nothing was more important to the royal family than American money increased. Many felt that the ways of Islam were forgotten by the rich and the ruling class and that the al-Sauds were becoming the puppets of the Americans.

The al-Sauds did nothing to change the public's perception of them. In fact, they did things that only made it worse. The Saudi government responded brutally to public criticism. Dissidents were arrested and imprisoned without trial. People were held in jail without charges filed against them. The police beat people in the streets, and some people were even executed. At a time when many saw Islam as being gravely threatened, the al-Sauds responded with Muslim-on-Muslim violence.

This only further proved to the people that their government had abandoned them.

Bloodshed in Mecca

In late 1979, tensions in Saudi Arabia came to a head. That November, hundreds of heavily armed Islamic extremists seized control of the Great Mosque

The town of Mecca overlooks the sacred mosque seized by Islamic extremists in 1979.

in the city of Mecca. They took hostages and held control of the holy site for days. They demanded reforms in the government and a return to a conservative Muslim state, one that was free from the money and corrupting influence of the West. After several bloody gun battles that left hundreds dead and wounded, the security forces of the Saudi government took back the mosque.

This battle at the holiest of sites in his homeland had a profound effect on Osama bin Laden and his nation. The House of al-Saud was surprised by the surge of popular support for the militants and was humiliated by the bloodshed. Many Saudis began to more publicly, and angrily, criticize their government. The view of the royal family as puppets of the West gained strength in the country. Though the political situation in Saudi Arabia eventually settled down, bin Laden had not forgotten what happened in Iran.

Bin Laden was vocal in his support of the militants and their cause, both during and after the event. To bin Laden, they were not only men who thought like him; they were martyrs and heroes. They had taken up the jihad and had been willing to die for it. According to a friend of bin Laden quoted in the *Observer*, Osama "was inspired by them. He told me these men were true Muslims and had followed a true path."[13]

Called to Action

In December 1979, an event took place that was to give Osama bin Laden his own opportunity to take up a holy war. That month, at the end of a year of tremendous unrest in the Middle East, the Soviet Union invaded Afghanistan. Previously, the Soviets had installed a Communist puppet government in Afghanistan, to shore up their influence in the Middle East. This government was eventually overthrown by Afghani revolutionaries. The Soviets, fearing the United States would support the revolutionaries, invaded in order to restore the Communist government to power.

Though at the time the Soviets were enemies of the United States, they were not Muslim. To bin Laden, that meant they were still enemies of Islam. The Soviet Union was a world superpower; Afghanistan was a poor, unstable country whose people were mostly peasants. In *Holy War, Inc.*, Peter Bergen sums up the shocked and angry feelings that shot through the Arab world: "The godless communists had taken a sovereign Muslim nation by force."[14]

As the Afghans struggled to fight the massive invasion, Muslims from around the world rushed to join the war. It was a cause that Muslims of all kinds could rally behind. According to David Plotz in *Slate* magazine, "The Afghanistan invasion...persuaded bin Laden and thousands of others of the need for Islamic holy war."[15] Twenty-two-year-old Osama bin Laden committed himself to joining the mujahideen, the holy warriors of Islam and Afghanistan.

Bin Laden had no plans to be a common soldier, but he knew he could be a leader behind the front lines. He had much to offer the mujahideen other than his religious fervor. The resistance would need money, and bin Laden had millions at his disposal. Though his family was wary of Osama's growing radical ideas, they joined him, and the rest of the Arab world, in their opposition to the Soviet invasion. Bin Laden knew his family and his family's wealthy friends and business partners could be counted on for support. The mujahideen would need to build bases, medical centers, and roads through the countryside's treacherous mountains. Refugees fleeing the conflict would need shelter. Bin Laden had already had experience in both construction and engineering, plus he had access to his family's huge supply of construction equipment. Initially he did not plan on picking up a rifle.

Only a few weeks after the Soviet invasion, bin Laden was on his way to

Jihad: A Word of War?

The Arabic word *jihad* is often translated as "holy war." The word conjures images of angry Arabs waving rifles and shouting slogans, or of the gruesome aftermath left by suicide bombers. As it is defined by Muhammad in the Koran, however, jihad has a much more complex meaning.

The term *jihad* can mean a literal holy war in which Muslims take up arms and battle oppression. Using violence to combat violence is deemed permissible by the prophet Muhammad, who is revered as a warrior. The Afghan resistance to the Russian invasion in the 1980s is a good example of this kind of jihad. *Jihad*, in its broader definition, however, means combating any force that threatens a Muslim's faith in his or her religion or their ability to practice their faith as instructed by the Koran.

The literal translation of the Arabic word *jihad* is actually "effort" or "struggle." This includes the struggle within oneself to remain faithful to the tenets of Islam despite the temptations and obstacles to faith that appear in daily life. In the Koran, Muhammad himself was careful to differentiate between what was to him the primary jihad, struggling with one's conscience, and the secondary jihad of a defensive war with outside oppression. This differentiation, and the Koran's strict rules concerning tolerance and the protection of innocents, has caused many Muslim leaders to reject terrorism as legitimate and righteous jihad.

Pakistan. Pakistan had become a gathering place for those assisting the resistance. There, bin Laden held secret meetings with Afghanistan's resistance leaders, Burharuddin Rabbani and Abdul Rasool Sayyaf, men who had visited his father's home.

Osama bin Laden had finally found a cause and a call to action. Like his heroes from the mosque in Mecca, he would join the jihad. "I was enraged," bin Laden later told an interviewer from an Arabic newspaper, "and I went [to Afghanistan] at once."[16]

Chapter Three

AFGHANISTAN: JOINING THE JIHAD

In early 1980, Osama bin Laden arrived in Peshawar, Pakistan, a lawless city thirty miles from the Afghan border. Already the main headquarters for the resistance, according to writer Jason Burke, Peshawar was "seething with soldiers, spies, gun-runners, drug dealers, Afghan refugees, exiles, journalists, and, of course, the thousands of sympathizers who had flocked from all over the Muslim world to fight the Soviet forces."[17] Peshawar's location near the Afghan border made it easy for resistance leaders to slip in and out of Pakistan. In Pakistan and Afghanistan, bin Laden learned many things and met many people who would greatly influence his future.

Joining the Resistance

It was in Peshawar that bin Laden finally met Abdullah Azzam in person. The two men, bonded by their beliefs in extremist Islam, took an immediate

Afghanistan

liking to each other and agreed to work together for the mujahideen. Azzam was already deeply involved in the war and welcomed the assistance and enthusiasm of the devout, and rich, young Saudi. Bin Laden was honored to meet and talk with someone who had so inspired him. Bin Laden remained in Peshawar for over a month, where he solidified his alliance with Azzam and planned for the future.

Osama bin Laden returned to Saudi Arabia in the late winter of 1980. His mission was to raise money for the mujahideen. Support for the

Afghans was strong in Saudi Arabia and bin Laden provided people with a way to show that support. Using his religious, family, and business connections, he raised millions in donations. He received money from his family and friends, from the Saudi government, from mosques, and from other wealthy and successful Saudis. Bin Laden also contributed funds from his personal assets, which were reported at that time to be at least $80 million.

That spring, bin Laden returned to Peshawar with a massive amount of money. Most of the money went right

Afghan students in Iran protest the Soviet invasion of Afghanistan. Bin Laden raised money in support of the Afghan people.

Religious leaders meet at an Afghan refugee camp in Peshawar, Pakistan.

into building an army to fight the Soviets. By this time, several months had passed since the invasion. Thousands of Arabs from countries such as Egypt, Somalia, Yemen, Algeria, and Tunisia were sneaking into Afghanistan and Pakistan to join the jihad and fight the invaders. The money raised in Saudi Arabia helped transport, train, feed, and arm these new warriors.

Behind the Scenes

In addition to millions in donations, bin Laden had also brought with him a few hundred tons of construction equipment, including bulldozers, dump trucks, backhoes, and cement mixers. These machines had all been donated by SBG, and bin Laden put them at the disposal of the mujahideen leaders. Under his supervision, the equipment was used to construct training camps for soldiers, dig tunnels, and build secret roads along the Pakistan-Afghanistan border. Refugee camps for those fleeing the war were built in Pakistan.

From 1980 to 1984, bin Laden and Azzam were an effective combination in supporting the resistance. They were respected among both the mujahideen leaders and the soldiers for their commitment to the jihad and their religious devotion. Together they brought money and soldiers to the conflict. Based in Peshawar, they worked as a team behind the front lines of the war.

Bin Laden continued his financial and logistical support of the mujahideen. He made many trips back and forth between Saudi Arabia and Pakistan, always returning with more money. Combining the donations, and some of

his own money, with his knowledge of building and engineering, he continued to pay for and oversee the construction of mountain roads and military bases for the mujahideen. He also built hospitals, refugee camps, and schools for Afghanis fleeing the war.

While bin Laden helped the mujahideen build, Azzam rallied support and recruited soldiers for the Afghan army. Azzam traveled throughout the Arab world and to the United States, calling Muslims to the jihad and announcing that the time had come for a

Afghan rebels on horseback set out on a raid against Soviet-held positions.

worldwide uprising. It was all beginning, he said, in Afghanistan. Azzam preached that "to stand one hour in the battle line in the cause of Allah is better than sixty years of night prayer."[18] New recruits poured into the Afghan army by the thousands. The recruits were from all parts of Islamic society, the rich and poor, university students and the uneducated. Many of them had only seen Azzam speak on videotape.

The Saudi Prince

During the early 1980s, bin Laden did much to establish his personal reputation as an honored and important figure in the resistance. At the hospitals he helped build, he visited the wounded. He praised their commitment and sacrifice. While he handed out small gifts, bin Laden would discreetly take down the soldiers' names and addresses. Then, only a few weeks after the visit, the wounded man's family would receive a large check. Bin Laden sent many checks to mujahideen families. Some checks were for things like shoes and watches; others were generous wedding gifts.

Bin Laden also used this time to spread his vision of fundamentalist Islam. He preached the holy virtues of jihad to the mujahideen warriors, promising them that their sacrifice would be rewarded in heaven. The war in Afghanistan, he said, was only the beginning of a long jihad that would cleanse the Arab world of nonbelievers. Bin Laden spent many hours at hospi-

tal bedsides and on mats in refugee huts, reading and teaching from the Koran. He even gave Arabic lessons.

Bin Laden inspired people with his appearance as well as his actions and teachings. He arrived at both hospitals and construction sites unannounced, often by military transport, and rarely told his name. He was a man who commanded attention and needed little rest. Through his dress, bin Laden demonstrated both his Arab roots and his wealth and power, even if that meant supporting a culture he condemned. Under traditional Afghan robes, he wore "tailored trousers of fine English cloth, and he always wore English custom-made Beal Brothers boots."[19]

For many, bin Laden became the example of a man rewarded by Allah for his devotion to Islam. He was a figure of wealth, power, and wisdom. Many called him "emir," an Arab title of royalty. Even those who had not met him knew of him and called him the Good Samaritan or the Saudi Prince. By 1984, Osama bin Laden had earned the personal loyalty of hundreds, if not thousands, of men.

House of the Faithful

In 1984, as the war raged on, bin Laden set up a guest house in a Peshawar suburb. Bin Laden named the house *Beit-al-Ansar*, Arabic for "House of the Faithful." Beit-al-Ansar became the place from which new recruits were funneled into Afghanistan. They slept

The Soviet-Afghan War

In the mid-1970s, in an effort to politically dominate Afghanistan, the Soviet Union helped Communist rebels assassinate Afghan president Mohammad Duad Khan. After the assassination, a pro-Communist government took over the country. Its rule did not last long as a coup deposed the Communists in 1979. The Soviet Union responded to this takeover by invading Afghanistan with more than thirty thousand troops.

Though Soviet military might dwarfed the Afghan resistance, the Soviet Union was not able to reestablish control of the country. The resistance received aid, through Pakistan, from the United States, Saudi Arabia, China, and Iran, all of which feared the expansion of the Soviet Union. The resistance was also helped by thousands of Arabs, like Osama bin Laden, who came to join the fighting on the side of the Afghans. Soviet forces were unable to conquer the rebels and the war became a stalemate, with heavy casualties on both sides. The Soviets controlled the cities, while the rebels controlled the countryside. The rebels were unable to muster enough force to take the cities, while the rough countryside confused and exhausted the Soviet troops. Popular support for the war in the Soviet Union eventually disintegrated. Finally, in 1988, Soviet president Mikhail Gorbachev announced the withdrawal of the Soviet forces.

The long war was costly to both sides. Five million Afghans fled the war to live in other countries, and over 1 million Afghans were killed. The Soviets counted fifteen thousand dead and over thirty-seven thousand wounded. The Soviet army never recovered from the cost of the war, and the Afghan tribes that united to fight the Soviets spent the next decade fighting each other for control of the country.

on the floor, a dozen to a room, while they spent several days meeting with bin Laden. Bin Laden lived at the house during his stays in Pakistan. While there, he held discussions with the men about the jihad, the evils of the West, and Arab history. He also led debates about important passages in the Koran. Volunteers bin Laden judged worthy were sent into Afghanistan to join the fighting.

At the same time, Azzam, with bin Laden's help, established the *Mekhtab al-Khadmat*, or Services Office. This house, located a few streets away from Beit-al-Ansar, became the administrative center of the war. All the field commanders for the mujahideen troops had offices there. Both bin Laden and Azzam published newspapers from the house. Together they published and distributed a magazine called *Jihad*.

They sent reports on the war and recruitment messages (via pamphlets, audiotapes, and videotapes) to mosques, Islamic media outlets, and Muslim schools around the world. Bin Laden paid the bills for most of the activities at the Services Office.

By 1986, bin Laden had moved to Pakistan permanently. He bought another house, this one in the expensive Peshawar suburb of University Town. From his two-story villa in the suburbs, bin Laden directed his expanding operations. He established several more guest houses in Peshawar. Bin Laden agreed to pay the living expenses of the families of men who came to fight the war, which amounted to $300 per year for each man. Working closely with Saudi intelligence, bin Laden was the primary director of funds being funneled from Saudi Arabia into Afghanistan. That figure was up to $20 million a year.

That year, bin Laden also became more personally involved in the combat efforts. He built his first training camp inside Afghanistan. Now, instead of just maintaining a place to help move men, he was helping train them in guerrilla warfare. From the base, he directed mine-sweeping efforts in the countryside. He helped mobilize the mujahideen by buying pick-up trucks and outfitting them with mine-detection devices and antitank weaponry.

Bin Laden also continued to help manage the logistics of the war. He

assisted in construction efforts along the front lines, digging trenches, roads, and tunnels. In a January 2000 article for *New Yorker* magazine, Mary Anne Weaver reported that bin Laden "often drove one of the bulldozers himself across the precipitous mountain peaks, exposing himself to strafing from Soviet helicopter gunships."[20] He also personally helped build a base in the hills surrounding the Afghan village of Jaji. Jaji was the village closest to the Soviet front lines.

Into Combat

In 1987, bin Laden became involved in combat. At the mujahideen base in Jaji, about fifty Arabs held off air and ground assaults by two hundred Soviet soldiers for over a week. Bin Laden was one of these men. Finally, after losing a dozen men, the Arabs retreated. Despite their retreat, the Battle of Jaji was declared a victory for the mujahideen. Never before had they held ground so long against a vastly superior force. Tales of bin Laden's bravery in the battle were published throughout the Arab world. It was said that he had taken the rifle he carried from a Russian soldier in hand-to-hand combat. He became a legend to the mujahideen and Muslims around the world.

Over the next two years, bin Laden remained involved in the ground war. While fighting in the siege of Jalalabad, he was injured by shrapnel. He fought in the battle at ali-Khel, one of

Afghanistan: Forever a Battleground

The history of Afghanistan is dominated by war. Though it sits in a mountainous area known for forbidding terrain, Afghanistan's location has always been important. It is a gateway between the Middle East and Asia. By linking the Middle East to Asia, Afghanistan connects Europe to Asia. Trade with Asia has been an important part of both European and Arabian economies throughout history.

Resident tribal cultures in Afghanistan were subjugated by the invasion of King Darius I of Persia in 500 B.C. About a century and a half later, the same areas were conquered by the famous Alexander the Great. After Alexander's death, various tribes traded control of the region. The Kushan dynasty ruled the longest and brought Buddhism into the area. When Islam came to Afghanistan in the seventh century, a line of Muslim rulers began that lasted over one thousand years. In the 1700s, Ahmad Shah of the Durrani dynasty, a powerful Muslim tribe, united the territory inside what are now Afghanistan's modern borders. Many Afghans still refer to themselves as "Durrani."

Throughout the 1800s and into the twenthieth century, control of Afghanistan was fought over not by Muslim tribal leaders but by Britain and Russia, both of whom wanted to control access to India. Britain was able to dominate the conflict and the country. Three wars were fought in Afghanistan during that century. The last, which ended in 1919, won Afghanistan independence from Britain.

Afghanistan was mostly peaceful until the 1970s, when economic crises forced the country to seek foreign aid. The United States and the Soviet Union, then bitter enemies, competed for influence in the region. When social unrest threatened a Soviet-supported government, the Soviet Union invaded Afghanistan in 1979. This started the ten-year war that introduced and involved Osama bin Laden in international conflicts. Afghanistan has been without a strong central government and has been torn by civil war since the late 1970s.

The forbidding terrain of Afghanistan has been the site of many wars.

the largest battles of the war. When not in combat, bin Laden continued other activities in support of the war. He continued to raise money and continued to spend out of his own pocket. In the war's final years, he was spending $25,000 a month to support it. He also helped organize the distribution of supplies and settled disputes within the mujahideen leadership.

It was during his time as a soldier that bin Laden began to exhibit signs of ill health. At times, he would be overcome by weakness and be forced to lie down for hours. He was treated for low blood pressure and diabetes. Reports began to surface that he had a serious kidney problem. He was treated for his ailments and for wounds received in battle by Ayman al-Zawahiri, an Egyptian doctor who was treating the wounded mujahideen in Pakistani hospitals. Reports of bin Laden's medical troubles did nothing to diminish his growing reputation as a hero.

The Prince Becomes a Legend

Bin Laden's legend grew as the war continued. He was regarded as a near-saint for leaving his comfortable background to join the war. He became known as a fanatical fighter and an inspirational leader. Soldiers rushed to fight with him, anticipating the honor of dying as a shaheed, a martyr, by bin Laden's side. Even bin Laden came to believe that he was protected by Allah and could not be killed. In fact, in a later interview, bin Laden told *Esquire* reporter John Miller,

> Once I was only thirty meters away from the Russians and they were trying to capture me. I was under bombardment, but I was so peaceful in my heart that I fell asleep. . . . I saw a 120-millimeter mortar shell land in front of me, but it did not blow up. Four more bombs were dropped from a Russian plane on our headquarters, but they did not explode.[21]

It is not known which tales of combat bravery told about bin Laden are true and which are not. What is known, however, is the impact of bin Laden's legend on the Muslim world. He became an international hero. More recruits than ever came to Afghanistan during the last years of the war, drawn to the conflict with the Russians because of their admiration for bin Laden. Thousands of young men from across the world were willing to die for Osama bin Laden. When he announced his plans to eventually expand the jihad beyond Afghanistan, thousands swore to join the battle.

The Birth of al-Qaeda

In 1989, bin Laden formed an organization called al-Qaeda, Arabic for "the Base." Bin Laden's and Azzam's recruiting efforts had attracted so many people that they began to fear infiltration

Afghan rebels in a machine-gun nest fire at Soviet aircraft in 1985. The Soviets finally withdrew their troops from the country in 1989.

by enemy spies. Also, they wanted a way to provide documentation for the families of the volunteers, many of whom came from across the globe. Al-Qaeda was a way to keep track of people's movements and keep those people who were trusted separate from suspicious persons. It became an "inner circle" that surrounded and protected bin Laden and Azzam.

When the Soviets withdrew their troops from Afghanistan in 1989, the purposes of al-Qaeda were expanded. The long war had seriously depleted the Soviet Union's military and economic resources. With the Russians gone, al-Qaeda soon became the organization through which bin Laden would expand the jihad beyond Afghanistan. Bin Laden was determined not to let his influence in the Muslim world go to waste. He recruited his favorite soldiers from the war for membership in the organization. Al-Qaeda took over secret camps used to train the mujahideen and made them terrorist training camps. In a matter of months, al-Qaeda was not only a military organization but had financial offices and a media committee as well.

After the War

The retreat of the Soviets made bin Laden fearless. He had at his disposal an army of nearly three thousand men. At the time of the Afghan war, the Soviet Union was a world superpower. Its defeat in Afghanistan destroyed the idea of a superpower in bin Laden's mind. "After our victory in Afghanistan and the defeat of the oppressors who had killed millions of Muslims," bin Laden told PBS reporter John Miller, "the legend about the invincibility of the superpowers vanished."[22]

Bin Laden was convinced that no army, no nation, could defeat him as long as he fought hard and long enough. The defeat of the Soviets, he claimed, was a warning to all those

The Cold War

Today, it is very difficult to imagine Osama bin Laden and the United States on the same side, as they were in the Soviet-Afghan war. However, the world political situation was very different in the 1980s than it is today. In the '80s, the United States was still deeply involved in a struggle known as the Cold War.

The Cold War was a time of great conflict between the United States and the Soviet Union. Both had many allies and were divided by the differing political philosophies of democracy and communism. Though the two nations, then the world's two great superpowers, never directly went to war with each other, they were involved in a nuclear arms race and competed throughout the world for political, economic, and military influence in other countries. In the nuclear arms race, both sides had many nuclear missiles aimed at the other country. There were enough missiles to annihilate both sides many times over, so the world lived in fear of a nuclear war that many felt would destroy modern civilization. The Middle East was hardly the only battleground in the Cold War. The United States and the Soviet Union competed for influence in Europe, Central America, southern Asia, Africa, and the Caribbean.

The Cold War came to an end in the late 1980s and early 1990s as the Communist government of the Soviet Union collapsed and the country broke up into many smaller nations. The United States and Russia, the main country of the former Soviet Union, now find themselves allied in many causes. One such cause is the war against terrorism.

who wished to oppress Muslims. "The Soviet Union entered Afghanistan in the last week of 1979," bin Laden said in an interview with *Esquire* magazine, "and with Allah's help their flag was folded a few years later and thrown in the trash, and there was nothing left to call the Soviet Union."[23]

For bin Laden, the spiritual experience of helping lead the jihad outshined the military victory. He has said that he never felt closer to Allah than when he was on the front lines fighting the Soviets. His personal survival and the Afghan victory over a vastly superior force convinced him that Allah had blessed the jihad. All Muslims, he said, should experience the joy of being willing to lay down their lives for Islam. In fact, the jihad was so inspirational to bin Laden that he brought his twelve-year-old to the front lines. Bin Laden did not want his son to miss the chance to be that close to God.

Back to Saudi Arabia

By the end of the war, bin Laden had made many valuable connections. Azzam had long been involved in an Egyptian terrorist movement called Islamic Jihad. He taught bin Laden about guerrilla warfare. Al-Zawahiri became bin Laden's personal physician. He too had been involved for years in Islamic Jihad. Bin Laden also befriended two of the mujahideen's most powerful warlords. With their protection, he was able to maintain his training camps. Though they eventually turned against one another, neither ever turned against him.

However, the end of the war also brought frustration for Osama bin Laden. He had hoped Afghanistan would be the launching pad for a worldwide jihad against the West. He found himself with little support, however, as mujahideen warloads who had been united against the Russians began to fight one another over control of Afghanistan. In Pakistan, the government that had supported him was overthrown and the new government did not welcome him. In November 1989, Abdullah Azzam, bin Laden's mentor and partner throughout his time in Afghanistan, was assassinated in Peshawar by a car bomb.

Bin Laden quickly realized there was nothing left for him to do in Afghanistan. Al-Qaeda continued to grow in secret, but a worldwide jihad would have to wait. At thirty-two, now a battle-hardened warrior and experienced leader of men, Osama bin Laden took his lessons, his legend, and his wounds home to Saudi Arabia.

Chapter Four

SAUDI ARABIA: "LET THERE BE NO TWO RELIGIONS IN ARABIA"

In 1989 bin Laden returned to Saudi Arabia as a hero. Despite their previous anger, his family welcomed him home with open arms because he had done so well in the resistance. The Saudi royal family, whom he had criticized in the late 1970s, forgave earlier insults and hailed him as a great citizen of the kingdom and friend of the family. He was considered a man who had, through his sacrifices and through his part in the mujahideen victory, brought great honor to his homeland, his family, and his faith.

At first, bin Laden appeared ready to take up a quiet life. He entered the family business with his brothers and started a welfare organization for veter- ans of the war in Afghanistan. By this time, bin Laden had a large family of his own that already consisted of four wives and ten children. He even made friends with some of the Saudi ruling family. This quiet front, however, was deceptive. Soon, another war would bring a new enemy to Saudi Arabia, turning bin Laden away from his family, his home nation, and the United States.

A Popular Hero

Upon his return, bin Laden became a popular public speaker throughout Saudi Arabia. Despite the fact that many of his speeches criticized the al-Saud family, the government allowed him to continue speaking. Since bin Laden was revered as a hero because of his time in the Afghan jihad, the Saudi royal family was reluctant to silence him. The close relationship between the al-Sauds and the bin Laden family also protected him. As he toured the country giving speeches, his speeches were taped, and thousands of copies circulated throughout Saudi Arabia. Thousands of Muslims were discovering bin Laden just as bin Laden had discovered Abdullah Azzam more than a decade before.

One major theme of bin Laden's speeches was the continuation of the jihad. Afghanistan was not an isolated incident, he said, but the beginning of a movement destined to spread across the world. The Muslim victory, in the face of a far superior force, was touted as proof that Allah supported and blessed the jihad. Like his teachers had taught him, bin Laden insisted that jihad was the obligation of every single Muslim in the world. Muslims remained in conflict with "the oppressors" all over the world, he said, and they must continue to be supported.

Jihad was not bin Laden's only controversial subject. He also demanded the destruction of Israel, insisting that Jews be expelled from the Middle East and their land returned to the Palestinians. He openly supported the Palestinian infitada, the terrorist war against Israel. Bin Laden also made anti-American statements, calling for a Saudi boycott of American goods as a protest against U.S. support for Israel. He declared the Saudi government as corrupt and un-Islamic, and he demanded reforms—by violent means, if necessary.

Calls for Calm

When bin Laden began to openly support Saudi opposition groups, his family and the Saudi government sought to quiet him. His brothers urged him to consider the damage he was doing to the family name. They encouraged him to focus on business and his own family. Bin Laden's friends in the Saudi royal family, including the governor of Riyadh and the chief of Saudi intelligence, now threatened him with public humiliation and possibly jail. In an effort to embarrass and discredit bin Laden in front of his supporters, a Saudi prince mentioned how close the al-Sauds and the bin Ladens had always been.

For a short time, the mixture of cajoling and threats seemed to work. Bin Laden made fewer speeches, though his tapes were still widely circulated and very popular. He concentrated most of his efforts on his private business holdings, expanding his business interests. Through investment and ownership, bin Laden became involved in thirty different companies outside SBG. He began to replenish some of the money he had spent in Afghanistan and created a large income for himself, independent of SBG. He was, in short, preparing for a future that did not involve Saudi Arabia or SBG. A military invasion would once again change the course of that future.

Iraq Invades

On August 1, 1990, Osama bin Laden, the Middle East, and the world were again shaken by a military invasion. The Muslim nation of Iraq, led by the military dictator Saddam Hussein, invaded the country of Kuwait. Kuwait, a tiny Muslim country, was easily overrun by Iraq's large army. It took Iraqi forces only four hours to invade the country and unseat the ruling government. The Middle East was

Iraqi dictator Saddam Hussein in early 2001. He shocked the world in 1990 when he invaded Kuwait.

shocked by the aggression of one Muslim nation against another. When Hussein massed thousands of troops on the Kuwaiti-Saudi border, it raised serious concerns for the safety of the Saudi kingdom.

According to Hussein, the Iraqi invasion of Kuwait was justified. He claimed that scholars of history in Iraq had discovered texts that proved Kuwait to be a province of Iraq. Hussein main-

tained that he was not invading Kuwait but merely returning Iraq to its rightful borders. The troops massed on the border with Saudi Arabia, he said, were there to defend Iraq's newly reestablished borders. He also claimed that Kuwaiti oil producers were stealing oil from Iraqi oil fields. If Kuwaitis were going to act like Iraqi oil belonged to Kuwait, Hussein reasoned, then Kuwait should belong to Iraq.

The invasion had strong reper-cussions throughout the Western world. Kuwait is one of the Middle East's major oil producers. When Hussein's forces subdued Kuwait, Iraq seized control of 24 percent of the world's oil reserves. No one believed the reasons Hussein offered for the invasion. Many feared, in fact, that Saddam Hussein was trying to gain control of all the oil in the Middle East. If this was the case, then Saudi Arabia, another major oil-producing country, was indeed in great danger. Many Western nations buy their oil from both countries and feared that Hussein would cut off the oil supply. Meetings were called at the United Nations to firmly condemn the attack. Western countries, especially the United States, immediately began to consider a military response to Iraq's actions.

Bin Laden's Fury

Osama bin Laden also had a strong response to the Iraqi invasion. He rushed to the Saudi capital city of Riyadh and met with the royal family. He promised them an army of Islamic warriors. He had at his disposal, he said, a ready-made army of thirty thou-sand veterans from the Afghan war. Bin Laden insisted that his army, com-bined with Saudi military forces, was more than enough to repel the inva-sion, liberate Kuwait, and protect Saudi Arabia. Bin Laden was adamant that

Muslim warriors defend Muslim land. According to a study of bin Laden and al-Qaeda by the *Middle East Review of International Affairs*, "Bin Laden saw the opportunity for a cause that could recapture the glory achieved in Afghanistan—defending the holy mosques from invasion."[24] Bin Laden was shocked and insulted when his offer was firmly rejected by the al-Sauds. They feared an organized, empowered, and radical army with no loyalty to Saudi Arabia's government.

After rejecting bin Laden, the Saudi government turned to the United States for military support. The government of the United States agreed to assist the Saudis. The Saudi government's invitation to the U.S. military infuriated bin Laden. To him, it was inconceivable that the armies of unbelievers would be invited onto Muslim soil. And furthering the insult, the Americans were invited to defend Muslim land while two existing, capa-ble Muslim armies were excluded. Bin Laden was more convinced than ever that the Saudi government had turned its back on Islam in order to serve the interests of the West.

Operation Desert Shield, a military operation in conjunction with the United Nations, officially began on August 7, 1990. Less than two weeks after the Iraqi invasion and annexation of Kuwait, the first American air force jets arrived. To bin Laden, this was an invasion even more horrific than that by the Russians, and far worse than the Iraqi invasion. Over the next several months, the United States deployed over 300,000 troops to Saudi Arabia. The infidel armies were located only miles from Mecca and Medina. The arrival of U.S. forces would prove to be another turning point in the life of Osama bin Laden.

The New Enemy

The presence of American troops in Saudi Arabia made the United States bin Laden's number one enemy. He spoke out against the United States in an interview with American journalist John Miller. According to bin Laden,

> America has spearheaded the crusade against the Islamic nation, sending tens of thousands of troops to the land of the two Holy Mosques... meddling in [Saudi Arabia's] affairs and politics, and... [supporting] the oppressive, corrupt and tyrannical regime that is in

An American soldier is pictured during Operation Desert Shield. Bin Laden vehemently opposed the presence of U.S. troops in Saudi Arabia.

control. These are the reasons for singling out America as a target.[25]

Saudi Arabia is home to two of the three holiest sites in the Muslim religion: the cities of Mecca and Medina. This makes Saudi Arabia the holiest place in Islam. According to the Koran, the dying words of the prophet Muhammad were "Let there be no two religions in Arabia." The welcoming of American forces into Saudi Arabia was, to bin Laden, a direct violation of Muhammad's last command.

There are many other reasons bin Laden hated having Americans in Saudi Arabia. Bin Laden believed in a very strict form of Islam, the rules of which were contradicted by how the Americans lived. Most of the American service

The American Military in the Middle East

A cornerstone of Osama bin Laden's hatred of the United States has been the presence of the American military in Saudi Arabia and the Middle East. Since the Persian Gulf War against Iraq, the United States has maintained a large armed presence in the Persian Gulf region. There are three main reasons for this. The first is an attempt at controlling the still volatile leader of Iraq, Saddam Hussein. The second is the protection of American oil interests in the region. Bin Laden is the third reason the American military has not only maintained but increased its presence in that part of the world.

In Saudi Arabia, America maintains the Prince Sultan air base near Riyadh. From this base, American warplanes patrol the skies over Iraq. Support personnel for the air operations remain there, as do other troops involved in training the Saudi military. Air bases are also maintained in Turkey, Kuwait, and Bahrain. About one hundred fighter-bomber aircraft are deployed at these bases. All of these bases are used to patrol Iraqi airspace.

Bahrain is also the command center for the Navy Fifth Fleet, which patrols the Persian Gulf. There are two aircraft carrier groups in the region, one in the Persian Gulf, led by the USS *Carl Vinson*, and another in the Arabian Sea, led by the USS *Enterprise*. There is an army supply station in Qatar and another on the island of Diego Garcia. Both places are small, politically moderate Muslim nations. There is also a warplane refueling station in United Arab Emirates, and cargo planes are based in Oman, another small Arab nation near Saudi Arabia. Since September 11, 2001, the aircraft carriers USS *Kittyhawk* and USS *Theodore Roosevelt* have been deployed to the region. The *Roosevelt* and the other ships in its battle group carry a contingent of fifteen thousand troops.

Under bin Laden's form of Islam, women's lives are extremely restricted.

people were not Muslim but Christian or Jewish, two groups bin Laden hated and saw as enemies. They also consumed alcohol, which is forbidden to Muslims. The men did not have long beards and often worked shirtless in the hot sun. Men and women worked together. And women drove vehicles, wore uniforms, and performed many of the same jobs as men. Bin Laden's form of Islam has strict rules to separate men and women and keep women inferior to men.

Anger and Arrests

Furious about the American military presence, bin Laden refused to be silent. Still a popular figure, he toured Saudi Arabia, lecturing in mosques, schools, and homes. Tapes of his speeches continued to circulate. Bin Laden said that American claims to be acting in the defense of Saudi Arabia were lies. He preached that the arrival of the Americans was the beginning of an effort by the West to destroy Islam.

Saudi Arabia and the United States: Intimate Strangers

For the past twenty years, the United States and Saudi Arabia have maintained a complex relationship based on the economic and security needs of both nations. The foundation of this relationship is the vast amount of oil produced in Saudi Arabia. Most of this oil is purchased by the United States. Oil is the lifeblood of the American economy, and the United States buys most of its oil from Saudi Arabia.

The desire for a close relationship arose in 1973. In response to U.S. support of Israel in the Yom Kippur War, Saudi Arabia severely limited oil sales to the United States. The U.S. economy plunged into crisis as gasoline became scarce and expensive. The embargo only lasted one year, but in that year the price of oil rose from $3 a barrel to more than $11. In 1974, hundreds of billions of dollars flooded into Saudi Arabia.

The United States, still in economic crisis, encouraged Saudi Arabia to invest its new wealth in America. The Saudis invested over $1 billion in the U.S. Treasury Department. The United States then spent the money helping Saudi Arabia develop its exploding economy and change seawater into drinking water. Through the years, Saudi Arabia has donated vast amounts to American charities and has been a major buyer of U.S. military equipment. The United States continues to provide economic and scientific services to the Saudis as well as military training. It provides Saudi Arabia with military security in a hostile section of the world.

Although the economic structure of Saudi Arabia resembles that of the United States, the countries' political structures could not be more different. Saudi Arabia is a monarchy that forbids free speech and denies many political rights. Women are brutally subjugated, and execution, usually by public beheading, is the punishment for a wide variety of crimes. In efforts to preserve the relationship, the United States has been delicate in discussing human rights with Saudi Arabia. Many Saudis are horrified by American society, which they see as lawless and immoral.

Since violence reerupted between Palestinians and Israelis in the past couple of years, the relationship has again become increasingly strained. The United States continues to support Israeli security. Saudi Arabia feels that the United States does this while ignoring the plight of the Palestinians, whom the Saudis support. As a result, the Saudis have become less tolerant of the American military forces stationed in their land, and the United States has looked to home-drilling, Russia, and Venezuela as alternate sources of oil.

As he had with Azzam in Afghanistan, bin Laden called on religious leaders for support. Since he believed the jihad to be a spiritual as well as military undertaking, it was important to bin Laden to have the backing of religious authorities. Two radical Muslim clerics, Safar al-Hawali and Salman al-'Auda, supported bin Laden in their own pulpits. In one sermon al-Hawali said, "What is happening in the Gulf is part of a larger Western design to dominate the whole Arab and Western world."[26] Bin Laden used the words of these clerics to support his own interpretations of the Koran and Islamic law. When Muslim leaders criticized him, bin Laden accused them of working for the West.

Bin Laden also spoke out against the Saudi government. He declared them "apostate," which means they had fallen away from Islam and become corrupt. Being apostate was worse than being a non-Muslim. Bin Laden abandoned his appeals for reform and began to call for the expulsion of Americans from the Middle East and for a violent overthrow of the Saudi government. The al-Saud family no longer cared about Islam, bin Laden claimed, but cared only about money and power. Bin Laden said it was a lesson they had learned from dealing with the United States. According to bin Laden, "This big mistake by the Saudi regime of inviting the American troops revealed their deception. They had given their support to nations that were fighting against Muslims.... The Saudi regime lost its legitimacy."[27]

The Saudi government soon tired of bin Laden's radical activities. They feared his popularity and wanted to maintain a good relationship with the United States. As a warning to bin Laden, al-Hawali and al-'Auda were thrown in jail. Saudi police raided bin Laden's home. He was put under house arrest and forbidden to leave his home city of Jeddah for any reason. Many of his financial assets and bank accounts were frozen or watched by the government. The al-Saud family strongly encouraged the bin Ladens to control their wayward member. While bin Laden's family and his government sought to contain him, bin Laden's organization in Afghanistan, al-Qaeda, continued to grow under his leadership.

Al-Qaeda in America

In 1991, bin Laden had al-Qaeda involved in a number of activities. Recruitment remained a priority. Volunteers for bin Laden's jihad were funneled into the terrorist training camps al-Qaeda maintained in Afghanistan. Soldiers trained by al-Qaeda but not invited into the organization were sent to fight in Bosnia, Chechnya, and Somalia—anywhere Muslims were battling those people they considered to be oppressors. The more skilled recruits were trained as terrorists. Al-Qaeda

Al-Qaeda soldiers undergo terrorist training, as seen in this still frame from an al-Qaeda recruitment video.

also began forging relationships with other terrorist groups based in Egypt and Palestine, providing them with money, weapons, and training. Al-Qaeda operatives were dispatched throughout the Middle East and Africa to research targets for future terrorist attacks.

As active as al-Qaeda was in Afghanistan, it may have been even more active in the United States. During the Soviet-Afghan war, Azzam and Sheik Rahman, one of bin Laden's allies from Afghanistan, had established "Service Offices" in several U.S. cities. These offices, which had been used to recruit support for the Afghan jihad, were immediately absorbed in al-Qaeda when the war ended. Al-Qaeda's main office was the Alkhifa Center in Bay Ridge in Brooklyn, New York. From the outside, this office appeared to be a center for Islamic studies. Other offices were maintained in Atlanta and Chicago.

The Brooklyn office was run by Sheik Rahman. By 1991, the Alkhifa Center was run entirely by people loyal to bin Laden.

Several al-Qaeda operatives were established in the United States by the end of 1991. One such person was Wadih al-Hage, an American citizen who had been born in Lebanon. During his student years at the University of Louisiana, al-Hage became attracted to the jihad. Though involved in al-Qaeda, al-Hage lived what appeared to be a normal life. He was married, and he and his wife had a son not long after their marriage in Tucson, Arizona. Soon after the birth of their son, al-Hage and his family moved to Quetta, Pakistan, where al-Hage became more involved in his work in al-Qaeda. In Quetta, his wife worked in a hospital. Al-Hage told his wife he was doing charity work in Africa and Afghanistan. In reality, he was helping al-Qaeda establish a terrorist cell in the East African nation of Kenya. Even his wife did not know what he was doing.

Another operative working for al-Qaeda was Ali Mohammed, a veteran of the Egyptian army. Mohammed also served in the American army, where he taught at Fort Bragg, the training center for the American military's special forces. He too was married, as marriage had become the most popular way for al-Qaeda operatives to obtain U.S. citizenship. After receiving an honorable discharge from the U.S. Army, Mo-hammed set up what appeared to be an import-export business, shipping various goods to and from the Middle East and Africa. Under the guise of a businessman, Mohammed traveled to Afghanistan to teach al-Qaeda operatives surveillance techniques he had learned in the army. He helped research future al-Qaeda targets in Africa and traveled to Brooklyn, where he taught bin Laden's followers military tactics.

Preparing for Exile

In 1990, bin Laden was also using al-Qaeda to prepare his departure from Saudi Arabia. Al-Qaeda had developed a good relationship with the intelligence office of the Sudanese government. In 1989, a military coup had overthrown the civilian government of Sudan, and a military dictatorship was imposed. Hassan al-Turabi, the leader of Sudan's National Islamic Front, was imposing strict Islamic law on the nation. In 1991, with al-Turabi's blessing, a disguised al-Qaeda operative bought two farms in Sudan, one near the capital city of Khartoum and another near the seaside city of Port Sudan.

Bin Laden's preparations proved worthwhile. By the spring of 1991, the United States had driven Iraq out of Kuwait, but American forces remained in Saudi Arabia, supporting bin Laden's belief that Saudi Arabia had been lost to the West. Meanwhile, bin Laden was under close watch by the government and his family. He could not combat the "invasion" as he wanted. Al-Qaeda was active and growing under bin Laden's command, and he needed freedom to continue.

Bin Laden's way out of his shrinking world in Saudi Arabia came from the government of Sudan. Having heard about the movements against bin Laden, al-Turabi sent bin Laden a secret invitation to come live freely in Sudan. Bin Laden convinced the Saudi government that he had to go to Pakistan on business. In April 1991, he sent his family a letter saying he was not returning to Saudi Arabia. Soon after, he arrived in Sudan. In 1989, Osama bin Laden had arrived home to Saudi Arabia a hero. Two years later, he abandoned Saudi Arabia as an enemy of the state.

Chapter Five

SUDAN: ONE MAN'S ARMY

Bin Laden's move to Sudan liberated him. No one there kept track of his movements, his words, or how much money he spent. No one interfered with his business, whether it was legitimate business or the administration and growth of al-Qaeda. In fact, the government aided bin Laden in his efforts. At one point, the Sudanese government provided two hundred fake passports for al-Qaeda operatives. It also granted one of his shipping companies a license to ship anything he wanted to anywhere in the world.

In turn, the Sudanese government benefited greatly from bin Laden. Bin Laden invested millions in banks, farms, and highways after his arrival. He also encouraged Saudi businessmen to invest in Sudan. He bought communications and military equipment for the National Islamic Front, Sudan's ruling party. The many companies bin Laden set up in Sudan to finance al-Qaeda provided thousands of jobs.

A Busy Businessman

In the spring of 1991, bin Laden started his family life in Sudan. He settled his four wives and several children in a large house in Khartoum, the Sudanese capital. They lived as the family of a moderately wealthy businessman. As he had in Saudi Arabia after his return from Afghanistan, bin Laden avoided material excesses. The two recreations he allowed himself were horseback riding and reading. After settling his family, bin Laden began establishing many businesses in Sudan.

Bin Laden's business ventures in Sudan grew to be extensive. He started

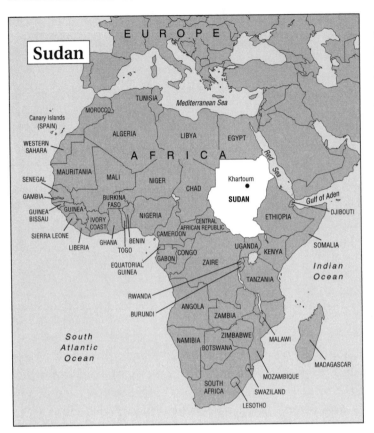

wasn't a single type of business in Sudan that he didn't have."[28]

As his empire grew, bin Laden was careful to maintain his image as a modest local businessman. His employees received health benefits. He made appearances at construction sites, where he was greeted by an adoring public, and maintained two large offices in Khartoum. Bin Laden brought a friend, Khaled al-Fawwaz, into Sudan to encourage Saudi investment in the country. Said al-Fawwaz, "When I observed [bin Laden's] house and his way of living, I could not believe my eyes. He had no fridge at home, no air-conditioning, no fancy car, nothing."[29]

a construction company, Al-Hijra Construction, that was co-owned by the government. Al-Hijra built roads and bridges throughout the country, employing hundreds of people. His tanning company exported leather goods to Italy. His farms covered millions of acres, employed thousands of people, and produced sugar, bananas, peanuts, sesame seed oil, and corn. Bin Laden also owned the trucking and shipping companies that moved his products. According to author Peter Bergen in an interview with *Atlantic Monthly*, "[Bin Laden] was one of the biggest businessmen in Sudan…. There

Bin Laden's Big Secret

Bin Laden's business empire, however, served a hidden purpose. That purpose was concealing the expansion of al-Qaeda. By the early 1990s, al-Qaeda had up to two thousand members. It remained a secret organization; only members knew of its existence. However, there may have been thousands more serving al-Qaeda's purposes, people who had no idea they were

Sudan

Sudan is divided into two main sections, north and south. The north is largely populated by Islamic Arabs. The south contains the minority of the population, which is predominantly of African descent. There is a strong Christian minority in the south, as well as followers of traditional tribal religions. Because of these racial and religious differences, the two regions of Sudan have been in conflict for many years.

The region that is now Sudan began as the ancient kingdom of Cush. That kingdom was part of the Egyptian empire and was influenced by Egyptian culture for a thousand years. By the sixth century, Egypt had divided Cush into three kingdoms, together called Nubia. Nubia, under the direction of Egyptian missionaries, became a Christian nation. Nubia reached the height of its power in the ninth and tenth centuries as an important source of ivory, gold, gems, and cattle for Egypt and the rest of Africa. By the sixteenth century, northern Nubia had become mostly Muslim. Nubia was conquered by the Muslim Turks of the Ottoman Empire, who ruled the area until the late nineteenth century.

In the 1880s, to protect colonial interests in the area, Britain established control of Nubia, then known as Sudan. It shared government of the region with Egypt. After World War I, the Sudanese people began to rally for either independence or union with Egypt. In 1952, Britain gave up its power over Sudan to Egypt. Egypt then put Sudan on a three-year schedule toward independence. On January 1, 1956, Sudan became an independent nation.

Independence brought trouble, as the Muslim north set out to suppress the non-Muslim south. Civil war raged through most of the 1960s. In 1969, a government representing north and south was formed. Civil war ended in 1972, and the south became politically and economically empowered. That power led to renewed oppression by the north. In 1988, the coalition government was disbanded and Sudan lapsed back into civil war. In 1989, frustrated by the impoverished nation and the ongoing civil war, Colonel Umar al-Bashir overthrew the government and seized power.

Though al-Bashir sat as the official leader of Sudan, power in the government was really held by the National Islamic Front. The NIF was led by Hassan al-Turabi. Al-Turabi insisted on the imposition of strict Islamic law (Sharia) not only in Sudan but throughout the Muslim world. Efforts to impose Sharia revived civil war with the south. Though receiving millions of dollars in foreign aid, Sudan continued to suffer from the ravages of civil war and drought. In desperate need of money and support for Islamic law, it was al-Turabi who brought Osama bin Laden and al-Qaeda into Sudan.

working for al-Qaeda. Many of its members were disguised as businessmen working for bin Laden's companies. Bin Laden's trucks, ships, and planes, the ones that moved his companies' goods, also moved money, people, and weapons for al-Qaeda.

In the early '90s, al-Qaeda expanded its financial reach around the globe. It collected donations in Europe, the Middle East, and the United States. It opened bank accounts throughout eastern Asia and Europe. It had offices in Hong Kong, Vienna, Croatia, and London. According to author Peter Bergen, "Al-Qaeda members bought trucks from Russia and tractors from Slovakia…and went on business trips to Hungary, Croatia, China, Malaysia and the Philippines."[30]

Bin Laden also used this time to expand al-Qaeda's military operations. Three new military training camps were built in northern Sudan. These were al-Qaeda's first highly specialized camps. They were used for explosives, surveillance, and assassination training. Only al-Qaeda's top operatives ever even saw the camps. Soldiers from the Afghan camps, as well as new Pakistani camps, were sent to fight in Bosnia, Chechnya, and Tajikistan. Weapons and cash were sent to terrorist groups in Yemen and Egypt. Explosives were imported into al-Qaeda camps from Iran. Information-sharing alliances were formed with Muslim terrorist groups in Egypt, Algeria, Libya, Yemen, and Syria.

Bin Laden also tried to expand al-Qaeda's capability for mass destruction. Attempts were made to purchase uranium in order to make bombs and gain nuclear technology. Al-Qaeda worked closely with the Sudanese government to try to acquire black-market uranium. However, they were unsuccessful in these attempts. Bin Laden also ordered research into developing chemical weaponry. Experiments were conducted with mercury and cyanide, with hopes of using these poisonous chemicals in assassinations. With help from the Sudanese government, al-Qaeda experimented with mounting poisonous chemicals on the tips of missiles and warheads. Al-Qaeda tried to purchase American-made, antiaircraft "Stinger" missiles. The handheld Stingers, rocket launchers that enable a single man to shoot down attacking aircraft, were effective in the Soviet-Afghan war and rumored to be available on the Afghan black market. Though al-Qaeda was able to purchase an American airplane in Arizona in which to ship the missiles, it proved unable to buy the Stingers.

Tutors in Terrorism

In Sudan, bin Laden worked with and learned from the leaders of long-surviving terrorist groups. Three such groups were the Egyptian group Islamic Jihad, Iran-supported Hezbollah, and the Palestinian group Hamas. These groups had long carried out attacks against

Israel, and Hezbollah had even attacked Americans. Bin Laden was able to convince their leaders that striking America was a way to strike Israel. In exchange for help with al-Qaeda, bin Laden had vast financial resources to offer.

Terrorism analysts believe that al-Qaeda first modeled itself after Islamic Jihad. Islamic Jihad, one of the oldest known terrorist groups, had long been active against the Egyptian government, which its members regarded as apostate. A large portion of al-Qaeda's leadership is Egyptian. Mohammed Atef, al-Qaeda's second military leader, was Egyptian, as was Abdullah Azzam. Islamic Jihad's leaders became close advisers to bin Laden. In fact, Islamic Jihad later became a wing of al-Qaeda.

Another group influential in al-Qaeda's development was Hezbollah. This group is backed by the government of Iran and based in Jordan. Hezbollah bombed the U.S. Marines

Palestinians demonstrate against Israel. Bin Laden has worked closely with Palestinian terrorists who have carried out attacks against Israel.

barracks in Jordan in 1983, killing 241 American servicemen. It is believed that Hezbollah leaders taught al-Qaeda how to bomb large buildings. The group is also suspected of having smuggled arms and explosives from Iran to al-Qaeda camps in Sudan. Payments for these services have helped support Hezbollah.

Hamas shared one of al-Qaeda's ultimate goals, the destruction of Israel. Because it has existed much longer than al-Qaeda, Hamas's already established terrorist network of operatives and hideouts was useful to al-Qaeda. Hamas operatives are considered by many the most fierce and dedicated of terrorists. Their main strategy in striking targets is suicide bombings. Al-Qaeda was able to give money and weapons to Hamas to fortify and continue its war against Israel.

Backing the Jihad

In 1991 and 1992, bin Laden and al-Qaeda acted in a supportive role, providing weapons, money, and training for other terrorist groups. They were not yet making their own strikes and took no public credit for terrorist acts committed in those years. In addition to supporting terrorist groups, al-Qaeda supported Muslim groups fighting in revolutionary, religious, or ethnic struggles. For example, nations such as Tajikistan and Chechnya were newly independent, having formerly been part of the Soviet Union. They had large Muslim populations that saw the instability in their countries as opportunities to control the new governments, or even to break away and form their own Muslim nations.

Bin Laden openly supported terrorist violence when he spoke to the press. He defended it as part of the jihad against oppression and encouraged it to continue. Al-Qaeda's European offices, disguised as charities or political support groups, had media committees that regularly spoke out in support of the worldwide Muslim struggle against oppression. At this point, Western governments, though they had known of bin Laden and his ideas since the early 1980s, were largely ignorant of al-Qaeda's existence.

Bin Laden, meanwhile, had lost none of his hatred for the United States. He resented the continued presence of American forces in Saudi Arabia and America's continued support of a corrupt Saudi regime. He criticized American-led economic sanctions, rules concerning what goods could be shipped into and bought from Iraq. The sanctions were designed to keep money out of Saddam Hussein's hands, since Western governments continued to see him as a threat. As thousands of Iraqi citizens struggled with poverty, disease, and starvation, bin Laden called the sanctions an act of genocide directed against Muslims. He also viewed America's support of Israel as an act of war against Palestinians and Muslims everywhere. In 1993, al-Qaeda began to support terrorist attacks on American targets and America itself.

Trouble in Somalia

In late 1992, the United States became involved in the war-torn country of Somalia. For years, Somalia had been ravaged by civil war, drought, and starvation. Various warlords fought for control of the country, destroying the government and the economy in the process. That December, America led a United Nations force that was created to help end the fighting in Somalia and allow humanitarian groups to aid the sick and starving. Bin Laden did not believe in the mission's humanitarian agenda. "Everywhere else [the Americans] have gone where Muslims lived," bin Laden said in an interview with *Esquire* magazine, "all they did was kill children and occupy Muslim land."[31]

American and other U.N. forces entered Somalia in 1992 with the goal of ending years of internal war and providing humanitarian resources to the beleaguered country.

In response to the mission, bin Laden began his first counterattack against what he saw as another American invasion of a Muslim country. It had been only two years since American troops had arrived in Saudi Arabia to make war against Iraq. Bin Laden issued an order for al-Qaeda to attack American troops in Somalia. He sent Mohammed Atef to Somalia to

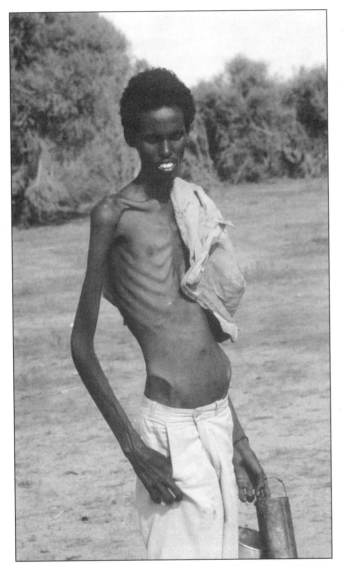

A young man bears the grim effects of famine in Somalia.

In late December 1992, bin Laden made his first strike against an American target. Al-Qaeda operatives bombed two hotels in Yemen that were housing American troops en route to Somalia. No Americans were hurt, but two Australian tourists were killed. Even after the attacks in Yemen, Atef continued traveling back and forth between Sudan and Somalia, supervising al-Qaeda's forces in Somalia and reporting back to bin Laden.

The First Attack on America

In early 1993, as American troops became involved in the fighting in Somalia, the American public was shaken by a terrorist attack on American soil. On the morning of February 26, a truck laden with explosives exploded in the parking garage of the World Trade Center in New York City. Six people were killed and more than a thousand were injured. Because of the size of the explosion, New York City authorities immediately suspected a terrorist attack.

research the best ways to attack American troops there. Other al-Qaeda operatives were dispatched to Somalia to win allies, bring weapons, and train warriors to fight the Americans.

The FBI began a massive, worldwide investigation in search of the bombers. It resulted in many arrests. The primary suspect was Muslim radical Ramzi Yousef, who was arrested in Pakistan after escaping the United States. Yousef was later convicted of the bombing and sentenced to life in prison. In New Jersey, the FBI arrested radical Muslim cleric Sheik Omar Abdel-Rahman. A bin Laden ally and terrorist recruiter working in the United States, Abdel-Rahman was convicted of planning the attack and also sentenced to life in prison.

The investigation uncovered ties between Yousef, Abdel-Rahman, and al-Qaeda. Yousef had previously organized a foiled al-Qaeda plan to blow up eleven American airliners over the Pacific. He had maintained an office in the Philippines that was discovered

during the World Trade Center investigation. Information that was to be used in future terrorist attacks by al-Qaeda was discovered on his computer. Abdel-Rahman's two oldest sons were found to be members of al-Qaeda. It was discovered that al-Qaeda, through groups such as the Alkhifa Center, had helped pay for and plan the bombing.

Though there were strong signs of al-Qaeda's involvement in the first World Trade Center bombing, bin Laden's exact role, and al-Qaeda's level of involvement, could not be determined. Midlevel al-Qaeda operatives, those who did not have direct contact with bin Laden, were authorized to participate in terrorist activities whenever the opportunity arose. These operatives answered to leaders authorized

The Secret Terrorist Factory

Although being trained in an al-Qaeda camp may provide preparation for carrying out terrorist attacks, it does not guarantee membership in the organization. One man indicted in the East Africa embassy bombing admitted to being trained in al-Qaeda camps but had never heard of the organization. He knew he was being trained for jihad, but he was not aware that it was al-Qaeda training him or that he was being prepared to play a small role in an al-Qaeda mission.

Most low-level operatives, those who assist in preparations and carry out bombings, are poor and uneducated. They are angry with the West, which they blame for their poverty, and seek the religious glory and purpose that they believe jihad will bring them. Those actually inducted into al-Qaeda are from a different background. They are generally middle class and educated, if not wealthy. They are more adept at strategy and technology and are less likely to be caught while preparing a mission.

to speak for bin Laden without having to directly speak with him. This strategy helped hide bin Laden's role in al-Qaeda operations.

Targeting America Again

In October 1993, al-Qaeda would again play an important role in attacking, and killing, Americans. That month, an American operation was launched to capture Mohamed Aidid, Somalia's most powerful warlord. It was hoped that his capture would help establish peace in the country. On October 3 and 4, American forces battled Somali rebels. The rebels shot down two American Blackhawk helicopters with rocket-propelled grenades. According to Mark Bowden, the author of a book about the American mission in Somalia called *Blackhawk Down*, the rebels had been given the grenade launchers and were taught to use them by al-Qaeda. Eighteen American soldiers and five hundred Somalis were killed in the fighting. A short while later, American troops pulled out of Somalia.

Bin Laden publicly celebrated the incident in Somalia. Since American forces left Somalia soon after the battle, he saw it as a victory not unlike the one in Afghanistan. Al-Qaeda had been involved in attacks on Americans in Yemen, New York, and Somalia. And at that point, beyond a few arrests, there had been no retaliation against bin Laden or al-Qaeda. This

furthered bin Laden's belief that there were no superpowers. He claimed there was great weakness in America. His criticism of the Americans, like that of the Russians, was fierce. Said bin Laden in a later interview with *Esquire* magazine,

> Our boys were surprised at the low morale of the American soldier and realized more than before that the American soldier was a paper tiger and after a few blows ran in defeat. And America forgot about being a world leader…and left [Somalia]… dragging their corpses and their shameful defeat.[32]

John Miller, the author of the *Esquire* article, summed up bin Laden's feelings about attacking a much larger, more powerful enemy. According to Miller, "Bin Laden had taken a swing at the biggest kid in the school yard and given him a black eye."[33] Encouraged by al-Qaeda's accomplishments, bin Laden and al-Qaeda spent the rest of 1993 researching American, English, French, and Israeli targets.

In 1994, some of bin Laden's plans for al-Qaeda were foiled. His Saudi citizenship was revoked and the remainder of his financial assets in the country were frozen. Two al-Qaeda assassination plots, one against the pope and another against U.S. president Bill Clinton, were discovered by U.S. and Saudi intelligence before they could be carried out. The United States used a combination of threats and sanctions to pressure Sudan into either handing bin Laden over to authorities for questioning about terrorist activities or expelling him from the country. In November 1994, despite revoking his citizenship, and under pressure from the United States to do something about him, the

Saudi government sent friends and family to convince bin Laden to come home. The invitation was refused. Bin Laden carried on with his activities.

Attacking the Apostates

In 1995 and 1996, two bombings connected to al-Qaeda occurred in Saudi Arabia. On November 13, 1995, a car

Osama bin Laden: Political Activist

Bin Laden's violent actions against the United States in the mid-1990s earned him international attention, but much of his attention was still focused on Saudi Arabia. While he hated the United States, he felt betrayed by his homeland. Bin Laden felt that Saudi Arabia needed to be saved not only from the United States but from its own leaders, the ruling al-Saud family.

After he settled in Sudan, bin Laden founded the Advice and Reform Committee (ARC). The ARC, based in England, was thought by many to be the political wing of al-Qaeda. Its purpose was to effect political, social, and religious change in Saudi Arabia. Bin Laden appointed Khaled al-Fawwaz head of the organization in 1994. At least in its public statements of purpose, the ARC claimed to advocate peaceful means of reform in Saudi Arabia. Because of its claims to support peaceful change, bin Laden was able to attract support for the ARC from powerful Saudi Arabians who were opposed to terrorism. A secondary goal of the ARC was to protect reformers in Saudi Arabia who were suffering at the hands of a Saudi regime famously intolerant of criticism.

A statement issued by the ARC in 1995 outlined many of the reformers', and bin Laden's, grievances against the Saudi regime. The statement said Saudi Arabia was too dependent on man-made laws when it should be ruled only by Sharia, Islamic law. It criticized how the al-Saud family lived in lavish palaces as the country fell deeper in debt (chiefly to the United States) and unemployment rose. It also decried the $60 billion the government had spent on the Gulf War and on its own military. If Saudi Arabia wanted to be safe, according to the statement, it needed only to return to the ways of Islam and give up the ways of the West. The statement closed with a demand that the king step down from his throne.

bomb went off outside the Saudi-American National Guard Building in Riyadh. Five Americans and two Indians were killed. The bombers were captured and admitted to being influenced by bin Laden's call for jihad. Three of the four men captured had served in the Afghan jihad. The investigation into their association with al-Qaeda and bin Laden ended when the men were executed by the Saudi government. On June 25, 1996, a powerful truck bomb exploded outside the Khobar military complex in Dhahran. Nineteen U.S. soldiers were killed and hundreds of others were injured. The Saudi government blamed the Hezbollah terrorist organization, but it also arrested six hundred veterans of the Soviet-Afghan war.

A photograph captures the devastation caused by a truck bomb that exploded in Dhahran, Saudi Arabia, killing and injuring many U.S. personnel.

Bin Laden was careful in what he said about the bombings. He admitted to having, along with other Islamic leaders, called for jihad. According to bin Laden, the bombers' success was cause for celebration and another victory for Muslims. He also admitted his words had influenced the bombers and went on to call them brothers, heroes, and martyrs. Direct involvement was denied, however, when bin Laden declared that he had missed the honor of participating in such a heroic mission.

Bin Laden viewed attacks on Muslim governments as completely justified. He hated the al-Sauds for allowing the American occupation of Saudi Arabia. He felt they had betrayed their Muslim subjects. He also hated the Egyptians for their attempts at peace with Israel and their friendly relations with the United States. Bin Laden struck at them as well. In 1996, a suicide truck bomb destroyed the Egyptian embassy in Pakistan. Fifteen people were killed and eighty were injured. In addition, al-Qaeda attempted to assassinate Egyptian president Hosni Mubarak while he was in Ethiopia.

Squeezed Out of Sudan

International pressure mounted against the government of Sudan. The governments of Egypt and Pakistan joined the United States and Saudi Arabia in calling for bin Laden's expulsion or capture. In Egypt and Pakistan, hundreds of suspected Islamic radicals were arrested and questioned about ties to bin Laden and al-Qaeda. Some were executed. Military and economic threats were increased.

Bin Laden began preparing to leave Sudan. In 1996, a group of radical Islamic hard-liners called the Taliban seized control of Afghanistan. This was the type of government bin Laden favored. In fact, he had given the Taliban $30 million at a key time in its efforts to seize power. The two sides began to secretly send representatives back and forth, considering the possibility of bin Laden moving his operations—business and terrorist—to Afghanistan.

In the spring of 1996, the government of Sudan announced that it was expelling bin Laden. It was a move designed to help improve Sudan's poor standing in the international community. Bin Laden had already finalized arrangements with the Taliban to move to Afghanistan and continue his jihad under its protection. Bin Laden left Sudan not in defeat but prepared to expand his holy war.

Chapter Six

BACK TO AFGHANISTAN: DANGEROUS SIGNS

In May 1996, bin Laden arrived in Afghanistan with his family. He was met by guards representing Taliban leader Mullah Mohammed Omar. Bin Laden was told that his role in the war against the Russians assured him their respect and protection. He first settled in the mountains of Jalalabad, where he lived modestly with his family, bodyguards, and advisers. For several months, he moved back and forth between several mountain camps.

The return to Afghanistan was significant to bin Laden for several reasons. Afghanistan was the site of his greatest victory, the expulsion of the Russians. The move also recalled an important journey of the prophet Muhammad. Muhammad was forced out of the holy city of Mecca by unbelievers. After eight years of war, waged in exile, the Prophet returned to Mecca as its conqueror. Bin Laden saw his exile, and his jihad, as a modern parallel to Muhammad's struggles. Lastly, bin Laden had settled in a country that endorsed his activities and promised to protect him. He now had more freedom to carry out his jihad than ever before.

Declaration of Jihad

On August 23, 1996, hidden away in a secret mountain camp, bin Laden issued a written statement called the "Declaration of Jihad on the Americans in the Country of the Two Holy Places." Believing Saudi Arabia had sacrificed its identity to the Americans, bin Laden would no longer call his homeland by its name. Bin Laden claimed, "The Muslims have realized they are the main targets of the aggression of the coalition of the Jews and the Crusaders."[34]

He went on to implore Muslims everywhere to take up the jihad. As he would continue to do in future statements, bin Laden made sure to mention two causes dear to even moderate Muslims: the fate of Mecca and Medina and the Palestinian conflicts with Israel. In his declaration, bin Laden made the following statement:

Our Muslim brothers throughout the world . . . your brothers in the country of the two sacred places and in Palestine request your support. They are asking you to participate with them against their enemies, who are also your enemies—the Israelis and the Americans—by

A religious protester in Pakistan displays his support of bin Laden's jihad.

causing them as much harm as can be possibly achieved.[35]

Though the declaration explicitly called for terrorist attacks on American troops, the majority of the grievances listed were against the Saudi government. Bin Laden still believed the presence of American troops in Saudi Arabia was as much a product of Saudi weakness as it was American aggression. He accused the al-Sauds of corruption, repression of reformers, and betraying Islam.

New Allies

During 1997, bin Laden solidified his relationship with the Taliban. As he did in Sudan, he used his money and influence to win loyalty from the country's leadership. He moved to the Kandahar region, where the Taliban was based. There, he remodeled an old Russian airstrip into a new compound for his family and his followers. He helped build a posh new home for Mullah Omar and a new mosque in Kandahar. Bin Laden bought weapons and cars for the Taliban. Because of his popularity with Muslims, bin Laden's loyalty to the Taliban brought many Afghan warlords, previously enemies of the Taliban, under the wing of his new ally.

Bin Laden also spent that year solidifying his terrorist network. Al-Qaeda established new training camps in Afghanistan and maintained at least two in northern Sudan. Bin Laden and

his advisers continued recruiting the best soldiers from the training camps into al-Qaeda. After swearing a formal oath of loyalty to bin Laden, the recruits became al-Qaeda operatives. Financial, military, and media "offices" were established. Each office director was hand-picked by and answerable to bin Laden. Bin Laden ordered al-Qaeda representatives to unify his organization with other terrorist groups.

In February 1998, bin Laden announced the formation of the World Islamic Front to Combat the Jews and Crusaders. The World Islamic Front declared the unification of terrorist groups into a worldwide alliance. Al-Qaeda officially merged with terrorist groups based in Egypt, Palestine, Pakistan, and Bangladesh. Previously, al-Qaeda had offered resources to other groups for their own attacks. Now, other groups would be helping al-Qaeda design and carry out its own plans. The goals of al-Qaeda became the goals of the other groups. They wanted to end Western influence in the Middle East, unseat apostate Muslim governments, and destroy Israel. Bin Laden called for Muslims around the world to join his cause.

Holy Orders and Holy War

An important part of his February 1998 announcement was bin Laden's issuance of a fatwa, a statement of religious importance and duty. In his fatwa, bin Laden accused America of aggression against Islam, citing the occupation of Saudi Arabia, war with Iraq, and the support of Israel as examples. In the fatwa, bin Laden shifted most of his anger away from the Saudis and onto the United States. America's threat to Muslims, he declared, went beyond the American military presence in Saudi Arabia. America has declared war, bin Laden said, against Islam:

> America has been occupying the most sacred lands of Islam.... It has been stealing its resources, dictating to its leaders, humiliating its people and frightening its neighbors.... It is using its rule in the [Arabian] Peninsula as a weapon to fight the neighboring peoples of Islam.... All these crimes and casualties are an explicit declaration by the Americans of war on Allah, His Prophet and Muslims.[36]

Bin Laden's hostility to Jews is mirrored in Indonesia, where a Muslim student displays a hateful sign.

With the United States now the primary target of his jihad, bin Laden expanded his calls for violence. The 1998 fatwa, published in Islamic newspapers, was an open declaration of war. For the first time, he called not only for attacks on the American military but for the murder of any Americans—military or civilian. Bin Laden's statements were the first by any terrorist group to specifically call for attacks on civilians. As stated in the fatwa,

We hereby give all Muslims the following judgment: The judgment to

The Taliban

In 1996, as Afghanistan's political leadership was in turmoil, a group of Islamic leaders, members of the fundamentalist Pathan sect, seized control of the government and imposed strict Islamic law. This group was called the Taliban and their leader was a man named Mullah Omar. Though the Taliban was recognized by Pakistan, Saudi Arabia, and the United Arab Emirates as the official government of Afghanistan, it never controlled more than 90 percent of the country. Ancient tribal law reigned in the country's most remote regions, and various warlords who one day wanted to control the country endured. However, the vast majority of Afghanis did live, and suffer, under the Taliban's strict rule.

Many new laws and restrictions were imposed by the Taliban. Men were required to grow their beards. Any man whose beard was deemed too short was beaten in the streets by the Taliban's police force. Women were required to wear a *burqa*, a combination of veils and robes that completely covered them; they looked out through a small screen that covered their eyes. A woman could leave the house only if accompanied by a male relative. Women could not own anything, work, or go to school. In addition, virtually all forms of entertainment were banned. Television, recorded music, and sports were all forbidden. Afghanistan's small Hindu population was commanded to wear a uniform that announced their religion. These were not considered new laws by the Taliban but a return to their version of Islam's original teachings. Problems such as a nonexistent economy and countrywide starvation and poverty were not addressed by the new government.

Under Taliban rule, women became virtually invisible under their *burqas*.

kill and fight Americans and their allies, whether civilians or military, is an obligation for every Muslim who is able to do so in any country. . . . In the name of Allah, we call upon every Muslim . . . to abide by Allah's order by killing Americans and stealing their money anywhere, anytime and whenever possible.[37]

The fatwa closed with a promise from bin Laden himself to lead the way by acting soon. It also became al-Qaeda's mission statement.

Bin Laden's announcement sent shock waves throughout the Middle East. Anti-American sentiment rose to new levels. Though most Muslims did not welcome violence, many felt they finally had a strong voice of their own in the world. They respected bin Laden for standing up to the United States. Supporters of bin Laden's extremism marched in the streets of Pakistan, waving posters that praised him and cursed the United States. Middle Eastern leaders, meanwhile, struggled to maintain peaceful relations with the United States, while at the same time not angering anti-American citizens in their own countries.

Support from religious leaders strengthened bin Laden's credibility throughout the Arab world. In March 1998, a council of twenty Afghan ulemas, Muslim religious leaders, met to formulate a response of their own to the American military presence in the Middle East. They soon issued a statement endorsing bin Laden's fatwa. Pakistani ulemas issued a similar statement of their own. The imam of Medina, the head of that city's Great Mosque, publicly declared his support for bin Laden while leading services.

Messages and the Media

During 1998, bin Laden also developed his use of the media. He had his fatwa, and other statements, published in popular Arabic newspapers. They were typed on a computer and distributed via e-mail. He began giving interviews with Muslim television stations and American journalists. In all interviews, he repeated his threats against the United States. Books published by al-Qaeda, with titles such as *Encyclopedia of the Afghan Jihad* and *Military Studies in the Jihad Against the Tyrants*, were now available on CD-ROM. Al-Qaeda operatives in Europe, disguised as fund-raisers for Islamic charities, were further encouraged to speak to the media and attack America with words.

A key component of bin Laden's publicity push was his use of Pakistani media. Though he was based in Afghanistan, bin Laden held most of his press conferences in Pakistan, speaking to Pakistani reporters. Aware of his growing support in Pakistan, bin Laden wanted a larger presence in that country's media. Pakistan was a more advanced nation, with better television,

Pakistan

In 1999, General Pervez Musharraf took control of Pakistan by staging a bloodless coup, replacing the country's corrupt democratic government with military rule. The move was popular with Pakistanis, many of whom had been impoverished by the deposed government. Since the change in government, Pakistan has evolved into one of the most modern Muslim nations, mixing Islamic traditions with secular life.

As Afghanistan's closest neighbor, Pakistan has always found itself embroiled in its neighbor's tumultuous history. Pakistan has maintained a powerful spy agency called Inter-Services Intelligence, or ISI (similar to America's CIA), that it has used to influence events in Afghanistan. ISI was deeply involved in Afghanistan's war against the Soviets. It helped recruits reach Osama bin Laden and join the resistance. It also helped the United States secretly support the resistance by delivering funds and weapons. In 1996, ISI helped the Taliban take control of Afghanistan; the Pakistani government believed that the Taliban would bring stability to Afghanistan. Stability in Afghanistan is good for stability in Pakistan.

Despite Pakistan's relative stability, there has emerged a small but vocal hard-line Islamic movement. This minority has led violent demonstrations in the city streets. There have been terrorist attacks in Pakistan, and the population fears there will be more. Osama bin Laden is a hero to the members of this Islamic movement. His name is spray-painted on city walls, and posters with his picture appear throughout the country. Just as many Pakistanis fought in the 1980s as mujahideen, so are there Pakistanis involved in al-Qaeda. Pakistan's hard-line Islamists openly support bin Laden's jihad against America. This places General Musharraf in the difficult position of respecting his citizens while maintaining Pakistan's positive relationship with the United States.

print, and radio services. The rest of the Arab world, and countries in the Western world, gained access to bin Laden's statements from their distribution in Pakistan. Most of the media outlets bin Laden wanted to use, especially television and computers, were banned by Afghanistan's strict Taliban government. Through Pakistan, he could reach the world's media without defying and insulting the Taliban.

Bin Laden also used media announcements to display the success of his organization. He continued his vague threats against America. On May 26, 1998, he announced that members of the World Islamic Front had been arrested in Saudi Arabia for possession of American Stinger and SA-7 surface-to-air missiles. He presented the arrests as a victory, declaring them proof that the World Islamic Front was succeeding in gaining new, more powerful weaponry. The arrests showed that bin Laden was able to place his operatives within the borders of his greatest enemies.

Bin Laden began holding interviews with the Western television media. On May 28, bin Laden gave an interview with ABC News, during which he said, "We do not differentiate between [Americans] dressed in military uniforms and civilians: they are all targets." He also promised "a black day for America."[38] Despite these threats, the American media paid much less attention to bin Laden than their Arabic counterparts. In America, bin Laden was still regarded as a man who made many threats but lacked the resources for strong action.

In his dealings with the press, bin Laden cultivated the image of a powerful military leader.

A Carefully Constructed Image

Bin Laden, as always, was careful about the image he presented. To the press, he showed himself as a powerful military leader—a great change from Sudan, where he had portrayed himself as a businessman. He arrived for interviews in a large military motorcade. He wore a camouflage combat jacket, carried a rifle, and was surrounded by bodyguards. Al-Qaeda soldiers would shout and fire rifles in the air to announce bin Laden's arrival. Bin Laden conducted interviews with his top military, media, and religious advisers seated at his side. He conducted all interviews in Arabic. His aides carefully screened anything that was filmed, forcing reporters to cut out anything that might help reveal bin Laden's exact location.

To his followers, the people that he lived with in Afghanistan, bin Laden presented a different image. When he visited al-Qaeda camps, he slept beside his men in their cave dwellings or in primitive huts made from branches. He ate the same simple meals as his men and prayed with them. He spoke only to his closest advisers about al-Qaeda's strategies, preferring to speak with the soldiers about the Koran or about their own bravery. Bin Laden spoke and carried himself with authority but lived modestly. This combination helped his men follow him as a leader yet still see him as a man that lived like they did. They believed that bin Laden jeopardized his own safety to be the public face and the public voice of the jihad.

Seeing into al-Qaeda

On August 7, 1998, at about 10:30 in the morning, two truck bombs exploded at U.S. embassies in Nairobi, Kenya,

Smoke rises following the bloody truck bombing of the U.S. embassy in Nairobi, Kenya.

and Dar es Salaam, Tanzania. Though the bombings were carried out in different countries, the attacks happened only minutes apart. At the Kenya embassy, 201 Kenyans and twelve Americans were killed. Nearly four thousand people were injured. At the Tanzania embassy, eleven Tanzanians and no Americans were killed. Each truck was driven by two men who were supposed to die a martyr's death in the explosion. One of the drivers, Mohamed al-Owhali, however, ran from his truck at the last minute and was captured in Kenya. One of the planners, Mohamed Odeh, was captured after he fled to Pakistan.

Al-Owhali's and Odeh's testimony gave valuable insight into al-Qaeda. Both men had received weapons and explosives training in Afghanistan and had been personally recruited into al-Qaeda by bin Laden. They had been sent to Africa at his personal command. Each man was sent to join an existing al-Qaeda cell that included surveillance, bomb-making, and computer experts. Neither man ever knew the other, or most of the other members of his cell. Al-Qaeda had planned the bombing for five years.

The most important part of each man's testimony was his admission to being a member of al-Qaeda. Those admissions proved that al-Qaeda was behind the embassy bombings. Osama bin Laden had publicly admitted that he was the head of al-Qaeda in his

1998 fatwa. And for the first time, terrorists indicted for their crimes admitted to receiving at least some orders from bin Laden personally. Although he had been suspected of being involved in attacks on American targets since 1993, for the first time bin Laden was directly implicated in an attack.

Bin Laden, however, denied any role. He praised the bombers and the bombings, as he had done with previous attacks on Americans in Saudi Arabia, New York, Yemen, and Somalia. He stood behind his own calls for further attacks on American, European, and Jewish interests. He said Americans had brought the attacks on themselves for their war against Islam. Yet he would not say that he had been personally involved in the attacks.

America Retaliates

Bin Laden's claims of innocence were ignored by the U.S. government, which launched its first military offensive against al-Qaeda and bin Laden two weeks after the embassy bombings. On August 20, the U.S. Navy launched cruise missiles at training camps in Afghanistan and a suspected chemical weapons factory in Sudan. Six camps and the factory were destroyed. Up to twenty members of al-Qaeda were killed. Bin Laden and his top advisers, however, had anticipated the attack and escaped. At the abandoned camps, the missiles destroyed little more than tents.

The United States also moved against bin Laden diplomatically. The Pakistani and Saudi governments were pressured to root out bin Laden supporters. Arrests were made in both countries. Pakistan was asked to find bin Laden and hand him over to the United States. The Pakistanis balked at being pressured to do what they saw as America's dirty work. Aiding the Americans would only add to the unrest in their own country. Prince Turki al-Faisal, head of Saudi intelligence, went to meet with the Taliban and bring bin Laden back to Saudi Arabia. Prince al-Faisal never made it past Mullah Omar. He returned to Saudi Arabia empty-handed.

Al-Qaeda Strikes Again

In 2000, bin Laden worked to personally establish a strong al-Qaeda foothold in the small nation of Yemen, the birthplace of his father. Yemen, with its weak central government, was full of terrorist operatives and armed rebel groups. Years of civic and political unrest had created a thriving black market for illegal weapons, from handguns to rocket launchers. Despite its unstable society, Yemen's port was an important U.S. Navy refueling station for ships in the Persian Gulf. Yemen provided bin Laden with everything he needed for his next attack: freedom, weapons, soldiers, and targets. He sent advisers to Yemen with orders to activate present al-Qaeda cells and research American targets. Bin Laden himself had married into a prominent Yemeni family.

In the spring of 2000, bin Laden selected an American warship as al-Qaeda's next target. Several al-Qaeda operatives moved into the waterfront neighborhoods surrounding the refueling stations. As they carefully watched the navy ships, they noticed that many small fishing boats cruised close by the warships without protest. Al-Qaeda packed a boat with explosives and piloted it toward a U.S. warship, making the boat the aquatic version of a car bomb. However, under the weight of the explosives, the boat sank.

In October 2000, bin Laden's organization succeeded in its next bombing attempt. On October 12, a small boat drifted up against the hull of the USS *Cole*, a refueling American warship. The men sailing it waved cheerfully to the American crew. However, the boat, piloted by al-Qaeda operatives, was packed with explosives and soon exploded. The explosion killed seventeen American servicemen and injured thirty-nine more. A huge hole was blown in the side of the ship, causing millions of dollars in damage. The dead and wounded were flown to American bases in Germany and the *Cole* sailed home for repairs. The FBI immediately dispatched a team of investigators to Yemen. Their investigation linked al-Qaeda to the attack.

Denial, Defiance, and Praise

Bin Laden continued his pattern of denial and praise. He again denied involvement in the attack but said that those who had carried it out were heroes and martyrs. Blame for the attack, bin Laden said, was on Americans and their aggressive policies in the Middle East. He was sure attacks would continue and that the damage they did would escalate. At the January wedding of one of his sons, bin Laden read a poem he had written in praise of the *Cole* bombing to a cheering crowd.

The Taliban kept its promise to protect bin Laden. Taliban representatives said they were convinced that bin Laden had nothing to do with the attacks. And they rejected demands that he be handed over to Pakistani or American

Yemen

From its earliest recorded civilizations in 750 B.C. until 1520, rule of the area that is now modern Yemen was shared by many groups of people, including the Romans and the Ethiopians, who brought Christianity there in 525. In the year 575, the Persians conquered Yemen. After nearly two centuries of Egyptian rule, Yemen was brought into the Turkish Ottoman Empire. By the time the Ottoman Empire conquered Yemen, Yemen was a Muslim land. It remained as such until the end of World War I, when the Ottoman Empire was destroyed. Britain and Saudi Arabia then shared, and clashed over, rule of the country until it was given its independence in 1934.

From 1948 until 1962, Yemen was ruled by various imams, men who served as kings and spiritual leaders. During these years, Yemen was rocked by a series of revolts and assassinations and had no stable government. In 1962, the military seized control of the country, declared a republic, and battled royalist forces. The two sides fought for five years, with the royalists receiving aid from Jordan and Saudi Arabia while Egypt aided the republicans. Foreign troops were withdrawn in 1967, but fighting and coups continued through 1972.

After a period of fighting between northern and southern Yemen marked by continued assassinations, Ali Abdullah Saleh seized control of the government in 1978. He declared a republic and was able to hold power for over ten years. The 1980s and 1990s were marked by repeated skirmishes between the government and rebels based in the south of Yemen. In recent years, the democratic government of Yemen has come to be seen as an elaborate disguise for an absolutist regime that is intolerant of dissent.

The gaping hole in the side of the USS *Cole* was the result of an al-Qaeda bombing that caused the death of seventeen U.S. servicemen.

authorities. A short while later, the Taliban declared that bin Laden had disappeared and that it had no way to contact him. At the same time, al-Qaeda completed construction on a new airstrip near Taliban headquarters. Supplies and recruits for al-Qaeda continued to pour into the country daily.

Bin Laden spoke of the *Cole* attack on a 2001 al-Qaeda recruiting video. "The victory of Islam has come," he said, "and the victory in Yemen will continue."[39] The "victory in Yemen," the bombing of the *Cole*, was not enough for bin Laden. He set about planning even more violent strikes against the United States.

Chapter Seven

ATTACK ON AMERICA: "THEY WILL BE TARGETED"

On the morning of Tuesday, September 11, 2001, four American airliners were hijacked while in flight over the United States. The hijackers, piloting the planes themselves, redirected the aircraft at three separate targets on the ground. All four planes crashed, and three of the four planes hit their targets—killing the nineteen hijackers, the passengers, and many people on the ground. September 11 was the worst terrorist attack on American soil. It was an attack planned, directed, and carried out by al-Qaeda and its leader, Osama bin Laden.

Since the attacks of September 11, 2001, bin Laden has disappeared. In the fall and winter following the attacks, U. S. armed forces searched throughout Afghanistan for bin Laden. However, they were unable to find him. For over a year, no one has been able to confirm bin Laden's location, or confirm whether or not he is even alive.

Tragedy

The first target hit was the World Trade Center in downtown New York City. The World Trade Center, near New York's financial district of Wall Street, housed thousands of office workers from across New York, the country, and the world. Its two main buildings, known as the Twin Towers, each stood over Lower Manhattan filled with smoke as the tops of both towers burned. Hundreds of firefighters, police officers, and emergency workers rushed to the scene to battle the fires, evacuate the buildings, and tend to the frightened and wounded. Firefighters began the eighty-five-story climb to the fires.

The second target hit was the Pentagon, the headquarters of the U.S. military, in Washington, D.C. At 9:43 A.M., the third plane, American Airlines Flight 77, crashed into one of the building's five sections, creating another huge fire. Again, emergency workers rushed to the scene to fight the fire, rescue the injured, and evacuate the building. The White House and the Capitol building were evacuated as a precaution, and Secret Service agents surrounded the White House. President George W. Bush, who had spoken of the "apparent terrorist attack"[40] from Florida before the strike on the Pentagon, was rushed to a secret location.

The tragedy continued to worsen throughout the morning. At 10:05 A.M., the south tower of the World Trade Center crumbled straight down to the street in a huge, roaring cloud of dust, debris, and smoke. Twenty-three minutes later, the north tower of the World Trade Center also crumbled. The jet-fuel fire had melted the buildings' steel support beams. That morning, over five thousand people who had been at the World Trade Center, as workers or rescuers, were reported missing.

The deadly al-Qaeda terrorist attack on the World Trade Center in 2001 stunned and outraged Americans, and much of the rest of the world.

at nearly a quarter-mile high. Offices, shops, and restaurants surrounded the towers. Several subway stations ran underground beneath them.

At 8:45 A.M., American Airlines Flight 11 crashed into the top third of the north tower. The plane exploded and its fuel erupted into a huge fireball, engulfing the top of the tower in flames. At 9:03 A.M., as thousands fled the first crash, United Airlines Flight 175 crashed into the top third of the south tower. That plane also exploded and started a terrible fire. The skies

The Firefighters

Among the very first people to respond to the September 11 attacks on the World Trade Center were New York City's firefighters. Hundreds were dispatched to the scene moments after the first plane hit. Hundreds were already there when the second plane hit.

The primary firefighting tactic of the New York City Fire Department (FDNY) is called aggressive interior attack. Firefighters rush into a disaster scene as soon as they arrive, getting to the source of the fire as soon as possible while maximizing rescue possibilities. At the World Trade Center, firefighters immediately rushed up the hundreds of flights of stairs inside the towers. As a result, several hundred firefighters were trapped inside the Twin Towers when they collapsed. The entire responding contingent of Ladder Company 4 was wiped out. Rescue 5, one of the FDNY's elite search and rescue units, lost over half of the firefighters assigned to that house. The FDNY lost 343 firefighters on September 11, 2001, in a matter of hours. That is nearly half the total number previously lost in the department's storied history. More than three thousand people were successfully evacuated from the towers.

As recovery efforts began in the United States, New York's firefighters became both national symbols and national heroes. On September 11, firefighters Dan McWilliams and George Johnson of Brooklyn's Engine 255 and Ladder 157 Company, joined by Billy Eisengrein of Brooklyn's Rescue 2, were photographed raising the American flag over the rubble. That photo has become the most revered image of the September 11 tragedy. Thousands of firefighters from across the country and the world spent months working in the rubble at the World Trade Center searching for victims.

A firefighter is overcome with emotion at the site of the World Trade Center attack.

Firemen, rescue workers, and others work amidst the devastation at the Pentagon.

By 10:10 A.M., the burning portion of the Pentagon had collapsed while rescue and firefighting efforts were still under way. Also at 10:10, United Airlines Flight 93, the fourth hijacked plane, crashed in an empty field in Somerset County, Pennsylvania. Passengers had overpowered the hijackers, but no one survived the crash. The true target of Flight 93, suspected to be the White House, the Capitol, or the presidential retreat at Camp David, was never discovered. More than three thousand people lost their lives on September 11, most of whom were still trapped in the Twin Towers when they collapsed.

The U.S. Government Reacts

The U.S. government reacted swiftly in case of further attacks. All flight operations within the United States were suspended. Tall buildings across the country were evacuated. America's borders with Canada and Mexico were put on high alert. Secretary of State Colin Powell returned from a trip to Latin America. International flights bound for the United States were ordered back to their airports or diverted to Canada. Five warships and two aircraft carriers were deployed from Norfolk, Virginia, to guard the eastern coast of the United States. The air force deployed fighter jets to patrol the skies.

The Secret Service continued to move the president around the country.

An investigation into the attacks began immediately. By 1:30 P.M., the president had promised to "hunt down and punish those responsible for these cowardly attacks."[41] The FBI reported that it was investigating the role of terrorist networks. Well-known terrorist groups such as Hamas and Hezbollah publicly denied any involvement in the attacks. By 4:00 P.M., the FBI announced that Osama bin Laden was a focus of the investigation. Within two days, Secretary of State Powell would declare bin Laden the number one suspect in the attack.

In mid-September, the United States announced that it was planning a massive and sustained military response.

The FBI and the Justice Department declared that they had hard evidence connecting bin Laden to the attacks. Several suspected al-Qaeda operatives were arrested in the United States. The goal of the military assault was to destroy al-Qaeda and capture or kill bin Laden. World leaders promised to support the United States as it struck back at al-Qaeda, bin Laden, and the Taliban. The United States proclaimed that an attack could be averted only if the Taliban surrendered bin Laden to U.S. or Pakistani officials.

Threats and Defiance

In Afghanistan, the Taliban remained defiant. Taliban leaders urged Muslims around the world to take up the holy war against America, and refused to surrender

Two weeks after the attack, a damaged fire truck sits amidst debris at the World Trade Center.

bin Laden. Taliban leader Mullah Omar warned the United States against an assault. Anticipating war, the Taliban stationed thousands of soldiers along Afghanistan's borders. In mid-September, the Taliban announced that it had again lost contact with bin Laden and had no knowledge of his whereabouts.

Bin Laden was unmoved by the U.S. threats. He spoke out through al-Qaeda media outlets. Said bin Laden on September 17, "We have been blamed...but we were not involved."[42]

When the Pakistani government promised to aid American forces, bin Laden asked Pakistani Muslims to rise up and combat "the American crusade." On September 25, bin Laden issued yet another threat. "Wherever there are Americans and Jews," he said, "they will be targeted."[43] Bin Laden remained in Afghanistan.

War in Afghanistan

On October 7, the United States led an international coalition in the first attacks on the Taliban. American and British warplanes began bombing Taliban troops and al-Qaeda camps. On the ground, leaders of an Afghani military force called the Northern Alliance, which had been at war with the Taliban since 1996, agreed to assist the United States and prepared for assaults on Taliban forces. The United States agreed to provide the Northern Alliance with weapons and tactical support on the ground as well as military support from the air. Northern Alliance troops would spearhead the fighting on the ground.

Throughout October, U.S. forces led bombing and missile attacks against al-Qaeda and the Taliban. The

Northern Alliance soldiers like these assisted U.S. troops in the fight against the Taliban.

Northern Alliance troops battled on the ground with support from commando raids by U.S. Special Forces. Little progress was made, however, as the Taliban surrendered little ground and continually refused to surrender bin Laden. It again reported to have lost touch with him. Al-Qaeda suffered heavy casualties, but a Taliban spokesperson declared that bin Laden was alive and leading his troops. At the end of the month, U.S. secretary of defense Donald Rumsfeld admitted that bin Laden had eluded U.S. forces and that he may escape Afghanistan before the war was over.

In November, the war turned. Warplanes bombed the Taliban and al-Qaeda as American commandos hunted al-Qaeda on the ground. On November 9, the Northern Alliance captured the city of Mazar-e-Sharif, a major Taliban and al-Qaeda stronghold. Three days later, the Taliban surrendered the city of Kabul, moving its depleted forces to its home base of Kandahar. As the Northern Alliance marched on Kandahar, the United States sent Marines into the Tora Bora mountains to fight al-Qaeda and find bin Laden. Kandahar fell to the Northern Alliance, effectively destroying the Taliban. Al-Qaeda forces were steadily defeated in Tora Bora and bin Laden was believed to be among them. Though most of al-Qaeda's mountain forces were eventually killed or captured, the new year saw bin Laden still at large.

The Evidence Against Him

There were a number of reasons for the United States to suspect bin Laden in the September 11 attacks. He had made many threats against the United States. He had said he would target civilians. Al-Qaeda had demonstrated a pattern of simultaneous bombings. The attack on 9/11 would have taken a long time to plan and al-Qaeda had planned previous attacks for years. Finally, significant resources of money, participants, and information were required. Only al-Qaeda was known to possess such resources.

In mid-September, the British government released a statement indicting bin Laden for a variety of terrorist crimes, including the September 11 attacks. The document details bin Laden's role as the leader of al-Qaeda and offers evidence of al-Qaeda's involvement in terrorist attacks as far back as 1993, including those in Somalia, East Africa, and Yemen. It also offers proof that al-Qaeda was behind the hijackings in America.

The British statement links bin Laden to September 11 in a number of ways. In the weeks before the attack, bin Laden announced in newspaper and television interviews that a major blow against the United States was coming soon. Al-Qaeda operatives were commanded to return to Afghanistan by September 10. At least three of the nineteen hijackers were members of al-Qaeda. One of them, identified through tapes from airport security cameras, was Mohammed Atta, a known leader in al-Qaeda. The report concluded with the following statement: "The attacks on the 11 September were planned and carried out by Al Quaida, an organisation whose head is Usama bin Laden."[44]

Bin Laden's War of Words

Bin Laden released his first extended public statement about the attack on America in early October. An Arabic television news network, Al-Jazeera, broadcast his videotaped speech. According to bin Laden, "America is struck by God in one of her vital organs.... Its greatest buildings are destroyed.... America has been filled with horror from north to south and from east to west.... These events have divided the world into two sides. The side of the believers and the side of the infi-

Bin Laden's War

Osama bin Laden declared war on the United States years before the September 11 attacks. Because bin Laden has wrapped his war in the robes of Islam, many believe he is waging a religious war. He has been careful to portray attacks on Muslims as attacks on Islam itself. Although bin Laden is repulsed by what he sees as a deeply immoral culture in the United States, he is fighting a political war.

Throughout his terrorist campaign, bin Laden has stuck to a strict agenda based on three connected goals: ending the American military presence in the Middle East, unseating the government of Saudi Arabia, and destroying the nation of Israel. Driving America out of the Middle East, he believes, will destroy the security of both the Saudi monarchy and Israel. In bin Laden's mind, all of his words and actions have served these three goals. He has not preached that Americans convert to Islam but that they end what he sees as their war against it.

The September 11 attacks struck at two symbols of what bin Laden feels drives the American presence in the Middle East: the economy and the military. The World Trade Center was attacked because bin Laden considered the Twin Towers the physical representation of the American economy. It was near Wall Street, and New York is widely recognized as the financial capital of the West. Bin Laden believes that it is the U.S. economy that drives American military policy. His second target was the Pentagon, the military headquarters of the United States. His past targets have been military bases, warships, and soldiers in the Middle East. The goals of bin Laden's "holy" war have been reiterated time and again in his many public statements.

dels."[45] He closed the speech with more threats, saying that Americans will not be safe from more attacks until there is a homeland for Palestinians and American troops have left the Middle East.

In mid-October, bin Laden spoke again of the attacks in an interview with Al-Jazeera. When asked about the Twin Towers being full of civilians, bin Laden said, "The towers are an economic power, not a children's school. Those that were there . . . supported the biggest economic power in the world. . . . We will kill their women and their innocent people." This interview marked the first time that bin Laden did not deny accusations of terrorism. He said instead that there are two kinds of terrorism: cursed and blessed. According to bin Laden, "Not all terrorism is cursed; some terrorism is blessed. . . . America and Israel exercise the condemned terrorism. We practice the good terrorism."[46]

On November 3, Al-Jazeera broadcast another videotaped message from bin Laden. At this point, bin Laden was aware of the worldwide coalition against him. He criticized the United Nations as a tool of American aggression and warned Muslim leaders against siding with America, claiming that those who do so "have abandoned the law of the holy book and the teachings of the Prophet."[47]

Important Revelations

Bin Laden's October comments revealed important things about his terrorist strategy. In both statements, he draws clear battle lines. One is either a "believer" or an "infidel" and their actions are either cursed or blessed. According to a report by the *Middle East Review of International Affairs*, "Bin Laden was demanding Muslims choose between supporting al-Qa'ida and thus taking the side of God—or being both apostates and . . . collaborators in the murdering of Muslims." In his black-and-white messages, bin Laden "defined al-Qa'ida as the representative of Islam and America as crusaders bent on a war."[48] Experts agreed that bin Laden hoped the attacks of September 11 would split the world into two sides.

The November video also provided information about bin Laden beyond his words. Although he speaks confidently, he confuses his facts. The United Nations did criticize him, but it had no role in the military actions against him. Bin Laden looks considerably thinner and older in the November video than he did in October. His beard is much more gray. This led analysts to believe that he was moving often and was in poor health. The video was taken as proof that bin Laden was in Afghanistan and that he was near the fighting.

"I Was the Most Optimistic"

None of these television broadcasts was as revealing as the amateur video shot by a bin Laden follower in November and released by the Pentagon in

Osama bin Laden, pictured with his son, divides the world into two groups: believers and infidels.

December. It had been discovered by American forces at an abandoned home in Jalalabad. The tape, featuring bin Laden discussing the 9/11 attacks with friends, was broadcast worldwide from the United States in December 2001. It contained what much of the world had been waiting for: bin Laden's admission that he was behind the September 11 attacks.

Bin Laden's comments throughout the tape prove that he had advance knowledge of the attacks, was involved in their planning, and had given the go-ahead for them. On the tape, bin Laden says, "We had notification since the previous Thursday that the event would take place that day."[49] He then talks about sitting by the radio on Tuesday, September 11, waiting for news of the attack.

After accepting praise for the attack from his friends, bin Laden says,

> We calculated in advance the num-
> ber of casualties. . . . We calculated

Bin Laden and the Muslim World

The September 11 attacks were well received in many locations throughout the Middle East. Rallies and celebrations in support of bin Laden and the attacks were widely publicized. Bin Laden is not alone in his hatred of America and his resentment over American foreign policy in the Middle East. However, although bin Laden's supporters receive much press, the vast majority of the world's Muslims are against bin Laden and resent the face he has painted on what is, for most of its followers, a peaceful religion.

Bin Laden and his advisers expected millions of Muslims around the world to rally to their cause in the wake of September 11. This has not happened. The actual number of people who openly support bin Laden may number in the tens of thousands, but there are more than a billion Muslims in the world. Every Muslim nation in the Middle East has sided with the United States in the War Against Terrorism. Hundreds of arrests have been made. Muslim nations that have not provided military support have provided intelligence and technological assistance. Muslim religious leaders have spoken out against bin Laden and taken great pains to speak to the world about the peaceful teachings of Islam.

Bin Laden, with his dream of a Khalifate, seeks to lead the Muslim world back into the distant and murky past. He has found relatively few Muslims willing to follow him. The most successful Muslim nations have been those that have addressed the difficult task of moving into the modern world while retaining the sacred traditions of their past.

Pakistani Muslims chant anti-American slogans. Some Muslims support the U.S. fight against terrorism while others oppose it.

the floors that would be hit....I was the most optimistic of them all...due to my experience in [engineering]. I was thinking that the fire from the gas in the plane would melt the iron structure and collapse the area where the plane hit and all the floors above it only. This was all that we had hoped for.

Later in the tape, bin Laden discusses planning the attack. "Muhammed Atta... was in charge of the group," he says. "The brothers who conducted the operation [the hijackers], all they knew was that they had a martyrdom operation....We asked each of them to go to America."[50]

Mysteries Remain
As of fall 2002, bin Laden had not been heard from again. There are many theories about what has become of him. It is widely believed he was injured in Afghanistan. In his last videotape, he does not move the left side of his body. This raises questions about injuries, since he is left-handed, or a possible stroke. Bin Laden's beard is gray in the tape, and he looks much older than a man of forty-four. American military commanders claim that bin Laden might have escaped into the mountains of Pakistan or even to Indonesia. He might also, they admitted, still be in Afghanistan. In July 2002, German intelligence maintained he was alive. That same month, an American FBI

agent theorized that bin Laden was dead. Neither source gave specific reasons for their assertions.

Catching bin Laden, if he is indeed alive, will be difficult. Several of his supporters did escape the American/ Northern Alliance assault on Tora Bora. Bin Laden may have escaped with them. If so, he probably moves daily, traveling with armed guards. He and his followers have stopped using the cell phones American forces originally used to track him. His last known location is in a treacherous mountain range.

Investigation and Pursuit
In the late summer of 2002, American investigators learned that several of bin Laden's bodyguards were among the al-Qaeda captives being held prisoner by the United States in Cuba. Bin Laden was very careful about choosing his bodyguards, selecting them for their loyalty and their willingness to die for him. Their capture led some American investigators to believe bin Laden was dead. The only way bodyguards would let themselves be captured, they reasoned, was if there was no one to guard.

The fall of 2002 also saw the continuing trial of Zacarias Moussaoui. During the September 11 attacks, Moussaoui was being held by U.S. authorities on immigration violations. Further investigation led to suspicions that he was to have been the twentieth hijacker on September 11. Moussaoui is charged with being a conspirator in the attacks. During his trial, he has admitted to receiving military training in Afghanistan, being a member of al-Qaeda, and being a follower of bin Laden and a participant in jihad. He is also known to have received pilot's training in American flight schools, as did Mohammed Atta, the leader of the al-Qaeda operatives involved in the 9/11 attacks.

As the hunt for Osama bin Laden continues, several things are known. Many of his top commanders have been killed or captured. Al-Qaeda military leader Mohammed Atef is dead. For the first time since he started al-Qaeda, bin Laden does not have a supportive country in which to base his operations. Millions in al-Qaeda's financial assets have been seized, and hundreds of its members have been arrested across the globe. Even though al-Qaeda carried out bombings and kidnappings in 2002, its ability to commit large-scale terrorist attacks, such as

that on September 11, seems to be destroyed for now. American authorities continue to assume bin Laden is alive and the largest manhunt in history continues.

When Osama bin Laden was born, it seemed that the path of his life had already been laid out, cut across the desert by his father's roads. It was to be a life of comfort, wealth, and big business. As a young man, however, bin Laden chose to step off the path set for him by his family and create a road of his own. It would be a trail from the deserts of Saudi Arabia to the mountains of Afghanistan, a trail lighted by hatred and marked in blood. In 2001, bin Laden marked America's doorstep with blood and fire. What road bin Laden will take next is unknown, but he walks it with his enemies at his heels. What the future holds for Osama bin Laden, a man without a country who started a war with the most powerful nation on earth, remains to be seen.

Notes

Chapter One: Beginnings: "Like Any Other Awkward Teenager"

1. Quoted in David Ensor, "Half-Brother Says bin Laden Is Alive and Well," CNN, March 19, 2002. www.cnn.com.
2. Quoted in Jason Burke, "The Making of Osama bin Laden," *Salon*, November 1, 2001, p. 3. www.salon.com.
3. Quoted in Burke, "The Making of Osama bin Laden," p. 3.
4. Burke, "The Making of Osama bin Laden," p. 3.
5. Burke, "The Making of Osama bin Laden," p. 3.

Chapter Two: University: History's Lessons

6. Burke, "The Making of Osama bin Laden," p. 4.
7. Peter Bergen, *Holy War, Inc.* New York: Touchstone, 2002, p. 50.
8. Quoted in Burke, "The Making of Osama bin Laden," p. 4.
9. Quoted in Bergen, *Holy War, Inc.*, p. 56.
10. Quoted in Benjamin Orbach, "Usama bin Laden and al-Qa'ida: Origins and Doctrines," *Middle East Review of International Affairs*, December 2001. www.meria.idc.ac.il.
11. Burke, "The Making of Osama bin Laden," p. 3.
12. Orbach, "Usama bin Laden and al-Qa'ida."
13. Quoted in Burke, "The Making of Osama bin Laden," p. 4.
14. Bergen, *Holy War, Inc.*, p. 51.
15. David Plotz, "What Does Osama bin Laden Want?" *Slate*, September 13, 2001. www.slate.msn.com.
16. Quoted in Mary Anne Weaver, "The Real bin Laden," *New Yorker*, January 24, 2000. www.newyorker.com.

Chapter Three: Afghanistan: Joining the Jihad

17. Burke, "The Making of Osama bin Laden," p. 4.
18. Quoted in Bergen, *Holy War, Inc.*, p. 56.
19. Weaver, "The Real bin Laden."
20. Weaver, "The Real bin Laden."
21. Quoted in John Miller, "Hello, America. My Name Is Osama bin Laden," *Esquire*, February 1999. www.esquire.com.
22. Quoted in PBS, "Hunting bin Laden: Interview with Osama bin Laden," *Frontline*, May 1998. www.pbs.org.
23. Quoted in Miller, "Hello, America. My Name Is Osama bin Laden."

Chapter Four: Saudi Arabia: "Let There Be No Two Religions in Arabia"

24. Orbach, "Usama bin Laden and al-Qa'ida."

25. Quoted in PBS, "Hunting bin Laden."
26. Quoted in Bergen, *Holy War, Inc.*, p. 81.
27. Quoted in Robert Fisk, "Talks with Osama bin Laden," *Nation*, August 21, 1998. www.thenation.com.

Chapter Five: Sudan: One Man's Army

28. Quoted in Bruce Hoffman, "Terrorism's CEO," *Atlantic Monthly*, January 9, 2002. www.theatlanticmonthly.com.
29. Quoted in Bergen, *Holy War, Inc.*, p. 82.
30. Bergen, *Holy War, Inc.*, p. 83.
31. Quoted in Miller, "Hello, America. My Name Is Osama bin Laden."
32. Quoted in Miller, "Hello, America. My Name Is Osama bin Laden."
33. Miller, "Hello, America. My Name Is Osama bin Laden."

Chapter Six: Back to Afghanistan: Dangerous Signs

34. Quoted in Bergen, *Holy War, Inc.*, p. 97.
35. Quoted in Bergen, *Holy War, Inc.*, p. 97.
36. Quoted in Bergen, *Holy War, Inc.*, p. 98.
37. Quoted in Bergen, *Holy War, Inc.*, p. 99.
38. Quoted in Bergen, *Holy War, Inc.*, p. 108.
39. Quoted in Bergen, *Holy War, Inc.*, p. 171.

Chapter Seven: Attack on America: "They Will Be Targeted"

40. Quoted in CNN, "Terror Attacks Hit U.S." September 11, 2001. www.cnn.com.
41. Quoted in CNN, "Terror Attacks Hit U.S."
42. Quoted in *September 11 News*, "The Evidence Against Osama bin Laden." www.september11news.com.
43. Quoted in *September 11 News*, "The Evidence Against Osama bin Laden."
44. Government of the United Kingdom, October 3, 2001. www.september11news.com.
45. Quoted in Bergen, *Holy War, Inc.*, p. 232.
46. Quoted in Bergen, *Holy War, Inc.*, p. 233.
47. Quoted in Reuters, "Osama bin Laden Excerpts from Al-Jazeera TV Broadcast from Dubai," November 3, 2001. www.september11news.com.
48. Orbach, "Usama bin Laden and al-Qa'ida."
49. Quoted in Bergen, *Holy War, Inc.*, p. 234.
50. Quoted in George Michael and Kassem W. Wahba, trans., "The Complete Text of the Osama bin Laden Videotape Released by the Pentagon on December 13, 2001," December 13, 2001. www.september11news.com.

GLOSSARY

emir: An Arabic title of respect and royalty, similar to a prince.

fatwa: A decree of a religious mission.

hadith: The sayings of Muhammad.

imam: The head cleric of a mosque and the religious leader of the surrounding Islamic community.

jihad: An Arabic term meaning "effort" or "struggle"; often translated to mean "holy war." It refers to the internal struggle to remain faithful to the teachings of Islam or to an actual war by Muslims against oppression.

Khalifate: A pure Muslim nation governed only by Islamic law.

Koran: The holy book of the Muslim religion, the writings in which were revealed to Muhammad by Allah.

mosque: A Muslim place of worship.

mujahideen: Holy warriors who fight in defense of Muslims and Islam.

shaheed: A martyr, someone who is killed in defense of Islam.

Sharia: Islamic law.

ulema: Muslim clerics and holy men.

FOR FURTHER READING

Catherine Broberg, *Saudi Arabia in Pictures.* Minneapolis, MN: Lerner, 2002. A photobook that shows the lives and landscape of Saudi Arabia in many color pictures.

Mitch Frank, *Understanding September 11: Answering Questions About the Attacks on America.* New York: Viking Children's Books, 2002. Written by a New York journalist who was an eyewitness to the attacks in New York, this book uses narrative and a question-and-answer format to discuss the attacks as well as the people behind them.

John Hamilton, *Operation Enduring Freedom (War on Terrorism).* Edina, MN: Abdo & Daughters, 2002. An overview of the current war on terrorism, focusing on events in Afghanistan.

Ann Heinrichs, *Saudi Arabia.* Jefferson City, MO: Children's Press, 2002. A general history of Saudi Arabia and an overview of its culture.

Bob Italia, *Afghanistan.* Edina, MN: Checkerboard Library, 2002. A look at the troubled history and contemporary culture of the nation.

Sue Penney, *Islam.* Crystal Lake, IL: Heinemann Library, 2001. A general survey of the religion, its history, and its influence on Arab culture.

Philip Wilkinson, *Eyewitness: Islam.* London: DK Publishing, 2002. A detailed look at all aspects of Islam as a religion, as a culture, and as a historical force.

Works Consulted

Book

Peter Bergen, *Holy War, Inc.* New York: Touchstone, 2002. A very in-depth look at the life of Osama bin Laden. Includes many primary sources and much history, including a detailed history and analysis of al-Qaeda. Bergen has studied bin Laden for years and is considered the preeminent journalistic authority on bin Laden and al-Qaeda.

Periodical

Edward W. Said, "Impossible Histories: Why the Many Islams Cannot Be Simplified," *Harper's*, July 2002. In reviewing two new books about Islam, Said comments extensively about the many strains of Islam and the history of the religion.

Internet Sources

ABC News, "Osama bin Laden: Suspected Terrorist Mastermind." www.abcnews.com. A basic, non-comprehensive report on the life of Osama bin Laden.

Jason Burke, "The Making of Osama bin Laden," *Salon*, November 1, 2001. www.salon.com. A detailed biography of bin Laden, focusing on his childhood. The article was reprinted from the *Observer*.

CNN, "September 11: Chronology of Terror," September 12, 2001. www.cnn.com. A timeline of events that took place in America on September 11.

———, "Terror Attacks Hit U.S.," September 11, 2001. www.cnn.com. An overview of the morning's events and the government's response on September 11.

Council on Foreign Relations, "Terrorism Q&A," June 19, 2002. www.terrorismanswers.com/groups/alqaeda.html. A basic history of al-Qaeda in a question-and-answer format.

David Ensor, "Half-Brother Says bin Laden Is Alive and Well," CNN, March 19, 2002. www.cnn.com. Brief interview with bin Laden's half-brother that discusses bin Laden's early childhood and possible fate.

Robert Fisk, "Talks with Osama bin Laden," *Nation*, August 21, 1998. www.thenation.com. An interview with bin Laden.

Bruce Hoffman, "Terrorism's CEO,"

102

Atlantic Monthly, January 9, 2002. www.theatlanticmonthly.com. An interview about bin Laden with Peter Bergen.

Robert G. Kaiser and David Ottaway, "Oil for Security Fueled Close Ties," *Washington Post*, February 11, 2001. www.washingtonpost.com. A detailed report on the history of U.S. relations with Saudi Arabia since the 1970s.

George Michael and Kassem W. Wahba, trans., "The Complete Text of the Osama bin Laden Videotape Released by the Pentagon on December 13, 2001," December 13, 2001. www.september11news.com. A literal translation of a videotaped conversation between bin Laden and several friends, obtained and translated by the Pentagon; the conversation includes a discussion of bin Laden's role in the September 11 attacks.

John Miller, "Hello, America. My Name Is Osama bin Laden," *Esquire*, February 1999. www.esquire.com. A veteran journalist's story about his 1998 trip to interview bin Laden; also includes information on the Taliban.

Carlye Murphy, "Bin Laden's Radical Form of Islam," *Washington Post*, September 18, 2001. www.washingtonpost.com. Brief article about how bin Laden's religious beliefs vary from more traditional and popular interpretations of Islam. Includes commentary from Islamic scholars.

Beth Nissen, "Police Back on Day-to-Day Beat After 9/11 Nightmare," CNN, July 20, 2002. www.cnn.com. Brief article about New York's Port Authority police officers in the aftermath of 9/11.

Benjamin Orbach, "Usama bin Laden and al-Qa'ida: Origins and Doctrines," *Middle East Review of International Affairs*, December 2001. www.meria.idc.ac.il. In-depth analysis of bin Laden's actions, philosophies, and beliefs as well as his goals for al-Qaeda. Includes a detailed description of al-Qaeda's organizational structure.

PBS, "Hunting bin Laden: Interview with Osama bin Laden," *Frontline*, May 1998. www.pbs.org. The first half of the interview is conducted by bin Laden followers. Journalist John Miller asks questions of bin Laden at the end.

David Plotz, "What Does Osama bin Laden Want?" *Slate*, September 13, 2001. www.slate.msn.com. A brief analysis of bin Laden's motivations for war with the United States.

Reuters, "Osama bin Laden Excerpts from Al-Jazeera TV Broadcast from Dubai," November 3, 2001. www.september11news.com. Translated transcript from an October Arabic television broadcast during which bin Laden comments on September 11 and the United States.

September 11 News, "The Evidence

Against Osama bin Laden." www.september11news.com. Provides translated transcripts of bin Laden's statements after September 11.

———, "Timeline: September–December, 2001." www.september11news.com. A day-by-day account of the September 11 aftermath until December 31, 2001. The site also contains consolidated information about Osama bin Laden and al-Qaeda gathered from numerous sources. Many AP and Reuters photos.

USA Today, "In bin Laden's Own Words," October 7, 2001. www.usatoday.com. Partial translation of statements made to Arabic radio and television by Osama bin Laden after 9/11.

Washington Post, "Osama bin Laden Excerpts from Al-Jazeera TV Broadcast from Dubai," December 27, 2001. www.washingtonpost.com. Translated transcript from a November Arabic television broadcast during which bin Laden comments on September 11 and the United States.

Mary Anne Weaver, "The Real bin Laden," *New Yorker*, January 24, 2000. www.newyorker.com. Article about the life of bin Laden, focusing on his years in Afghanistan fighting the Russians and in Sudan.

INDEX

religious development of,
17–18, 23, 27–29
speaks out against Saudi
Arabian government,
47–48, 55, 69, 74
bin Laden, Salem (brother),
16, 23, 26–27
bin Laden, Yeslam (brother),
23
Bin Laden Group, 12, 14–15
see also Saudi Bin Laden
Group
Blackhawk Down (Bowden),
68
Blackhawk helicopters, 68
Bosnia, 55, 62
Bowden, Mark, 68
Brooklyn, 56–57
Buddhism, 42
Burke, Jason, 19, 23, 25, 35
burqa, 76
Bush, George W., 86

Canada, 88
Capitol building, 86
Carl Vinson (aircraft carrier),
52
Chechnya, 55, 62
chemical weapons, 62
Chicago, 56
China, 40, 62
Christianity, 20, 29, 83
Clinton, Bill, 68
CNN, 18, 27
Cold War, 45
Cole (refueling warship),
82–84
Croatia, 62
Cush, 61
cyanide, 62

Dar es Salaam, 81
Darius I, 42
Declaration of Jihad, 72–74

Dhahran, 70
Diego Garcia, 52
Disney, 26
Durrani dynasty, 42

Egypt
Arabia conquered by, 14
in Arab-Israeli wars, 21–22
arrests Islamic radicals in,
71
Azzam expelled from, 28
Azzam's education in, 27
executes Sayyid Qutb, 28
al-Qaeda attacks against, 71
signs peace agreement with
Israel, 31
Sudan shares government
with, 61
support for Yemen by, 83
terrorist activities in, 56, 62,
74
Eisengrein, Billy, 87
emir. *See* bin Laden, Osama
bin Mohammed
Encyclopedia of the Afghan Jihad
(al-Qaeda), 77
Enterprise (aircraft carrier), 52
Esquire (magazine), 43, 46, 65,
68
Ethiopians, 83

Fahd, King, 26
al-Faisal, Turki, 82
fatwa, 74–75, 77
al-Fawwaz, 60
FBI. *See* Federal Bureau of
Investigation
FDNY. *See* New York City
Fire Department
Federal Bureau of
Investigation (FBI), 66–67,
82, 88–89, 96
firefighters, 87
Florida, 23, 27

Fort Bragg, 57
fundamentalist Islam, 24–25
Fyfield-Shayler, Brian, 19

Good Samaritan. *See* bin
Laden, Osama bin
Mohammed
Gorbachev, Mikhail, 40
Great Britain, 42, 61, 83, 91
Great Mosque, 32–33
Great Mosques, 14–15

hadith, 20
Hadramut province, 12
al-Hage, Wadih, 57
hajj, 18, 20
Hamas, 62, 64, 88
Hard Rock Café, 26
Harvard University, 26
al-Hawali, Safar, 55
Hezbollah, 62–64, 70, 88
highways, 15
Al-Hijra Construction, 60
Hindus, 76
holy war. *See* jihad
Holy War, Inc. (Bergen), 27
Hong Kong, 62
House of the Faithful, 39–41
Houston, 27
Hungary, 62
Hussein, Saddam, 49–50, 52,
64

Ibn Saud, 14
India, 42
Inter-Services Intelligence
(ISI), 78
Iran, 21, 30–31, 40, 62–64
Iraq, 49–51
ISI. *See* Inter-Services
Intelligence
Islam
arrival of, in Afghanistan,
42

visit bin Laden home dur-
ing the hajj, 18
women's rights among,
16–17

Nairobi, 80
National Islamic Front (NIF),
57, 61
Navy Fifth Fleet, 52
New Jersey, 26
New York City
attacks on World Trade
Center in, 66–68, 85–87,
92
terrorist groups in, 56
New York City Fire
Department (FDNY), 87
New Yorker (magazine), 41
NIF. *See* National Islamic
Front
9-11. *See* September 11, 2001,
terrorist attacks
Norfolk, 88
Northern Alliance, 90–91
Nubia, 61
nuclear arms race, 45

Observer (newspaper), 33
Odeh, Mohamed, 81
oil embargo, 54
oil fields, 49–50
Oman, 52
Omar, Mullah Mohammed,
72, 74, 76, 82
Operation Desert Shield,
50–51
Orbach, Benjamin, 30
Orlando, 27
Ottoman Empire, 61, 83
al-Owhali, Mohamed, 81

Pakistan
arrests of terrorists in, 71,
82

as gathering place for resistance supporters, 34
government overthrown in,
46
history of, 78
Osama buys houses in, 41
Osama establishes House
of the Faithful in, 39–41
Osama meets Azzam in, 35
Osama's use of the media
in, 77–79
al-Qaeda bombings in, 71
recognition of Taliban by,
76
supports Afghanistan, 40
terrorist activities in, 57, 74
Palestine
origin of, 22
Osama's support for, 48
Saudi Arabia's support of,
54
terrorist activities in, 56, 74
Palestinian Liberation
Organization (PLO), 22,
27
PBS, 45
Pennsylvania, 88
Pentagon, 86, 88, 92–93
Persian Gulf War, 52
Persians, 83
Peshawar, 35, 41, 46
Philippines, 62, 67
pilgrimages. *See* hajj
PLO. *See* Palestinian
Liberation Organization
Plotz, David, 33
Porsche, 26
Port Sudan, 57
Powell, Colin, 88–89
Prince Sultan air base, 52
Prophet, the. *See* Muhammad

Qaddafi, Muammar, 21
al-Qaeda

activities of
in Afghanistan, 74
in Sudan, 62
in United States, 55–57,
62
assassination plots by,
68–69, 71
attacks against Americans
by
on Blackhawk heli-
copters in Somalia,
68
on *Cole*, 82–84
on September 11, 2001,
85–92
on troops en route to
Somalia, 65–66
at U.S. embassies, 80–81
at World Trade Center,
66–68, 85–87, 92
bombings in Saudi Arabia
by, 69–71
expands worldwide, 60, 62
experiments with poisonous
chemicals, 62
founding of, 43–45
membership into, 67
mission statement of, 77
Osama's visits to camps of,
80
terrorist groups influential
in development of,
63–64
U.S. attacks in Afghanistan,
90–91
see also terrorism
Qatar, 52
Quetta, 57
Qutb, Muhammad, 28–29
Qutb, Sayyid, 28

Rabbani, Burharuddin, 34
Rahman, Sheik, 56–57
Ramadan, 20

Picture Credits

ABOUT THE AUTHOR

Bill Loehfelm was born and raised in New York City and now lives in New Orleans, Louisiana. After a nine-year career teaching high school English, he left education in 2000 to pursue writing full time. He graduated from the University of Scranton in 1991 and is currently studying for an MA in English at the University of New Orleans.

A portion of the author's proceeds from this book have been donated to the New York Police and Fire Widows' and Children's Benefit Fund.